NONE CAME HOME
The War Dogs of Vietnam

By

Sgt. John E. O'Donnell

ISBN: 0-75960-159-3

This book is printed on acid free paper.

1stBooks - rev. 06/18/01

PROCEEDS FROM THIS BOOK BENEFIT:

THE WAR DOG MEMORIAL & EDUCATION FUND

At

www.wardogmemorial.com

CONTENTS

PREFACE

Although dogs have been with humans throughout history, assisting and fighting side by side against all predators and enemies, K-9 as an organized fighting unit of man and dog did not come to military reality for the United States until the early days of World War II.

Until then, many organizations and nations throughout the world used dogs primarily in locating the wounded and lost on the battlefield or to deliver messages from camp to camp and headquarters to headquarters. Other uses, such as an early warning system against invading enemy attacks, a defense strategy since Roman times, and security, guarding important and strategic areas or personnel, also saw major duty.

Even though the United States formally acknowledged the effectiveness of a canine's superior sense of smell, sight, and hearing in forming its K-9 Corps. Very little has been written or said to acknowledge the contributions and accomplishments these dogs have given to this nation.. However, their heroic deeds are well known to the military and to the men whose lives have been saved by these heroic dogs and their handlers.

Dogs continue to do important work to this day, assisting humans in times of natural disasters and man-made calamities. Almost everyday on television one watches law enforcement branches and search teams utilize dogs in much heralded tasks: locating missing, earthquake or forest fire victims, apprehending escaped felons, and detecting illegal drugs or explosives. The President himself does not enter a room when on a mission outside the Nation unless a specialized dog team from the secret service has examined it. Most people don't even notice the workings of a good dog unit, yet these canine squads have been documented to influence a nation's emotional recovery in times of upheaval and distress.

It has been long studied that just the dog's presence has given aid and comfort to individuals. But where morale has been boosted, there are numerous documented acts of bravery these dogs have performed in the line of duty.

Stationed on the European front in World War II, a German shepherd named Chips singled-handedly forced two machine gun nests to surrender, saving the lives of countless soldiers. His thankful commander awarded him medals for his deeds and service but the Army took Chip's unit citations away from him after the war.

In the Korean War, York, a Doberman Pincher, led 154 combat missions and is credited with never losing a man from an ambush or explosive detonated "booby-trap". York however was never commemorated.

After these conflicts, the conventional wisdom in the military believed war dogs could finally be replaced by modern technology. Computers could now operate sensor and detection devices strategically placed on land, in the sky, and on satellites in space. The K-9 program, for all practical purposes, was thus dismantled and unceremoniously swept into the dustbins of history.

It was Vietnam that proved the military strategists wrong.

Under the insistence of General William Westmoreland and his staff, after studying the British war strategy in South West Asia, the military planners finally resurrected the K-9 program and made arrangements with the British SAS in Malaysia to initiate and instruct the Americans in the specialized training of dogs of war. This was a strange twist of events after it was the Americans, during the Second World War that helped initiate the British K-9 program.

In Vietnam alone, official estimates credit the war dogs with saving the lives of over 15,000 American military personnel and never allowing a successful enemy incursion or infiltration of an American air base or military installation throughout the course of the war, while they were present. In fact, so significantly did canines interrupt and upset the enemy's military tactics and strategies the vaunted Viet Cong found it necessary to place bounties on the head of both dog and handler.

Since the conflict in Vietnam, virtually every major paramilitary K-9 program in the United States has been modeled after the one drafted and used by those dog handlers. Today, this dog training system, divided from five categories: sentry, scout, mines and explosives, combat, and tracker, continues its dedicated service to the United States.

In addition, analysts can only estimate the casualties spared in Operation: Desert Storm due to war dogs who uncovered scores of booby-traps and other explosives left behind by Saddam Hussein army for American soldiers. Recently, K-9 units reasserted their necessity by rescuing a stealth pilot shot down in Bosnia.

Although the following story deals primarily with the Southeast Asian conflict known as the Vietnam War, K-9 has continually functioned as an incredible tool used to build morale and save the lives of the troops they served. The achievements these canines have amassed would bring anyone else the Congressional Medal of Honor. Every dog procured during this conflict was made from a donation by families and organizations answering this nation's call. Yet, the treatment these dogs received at the end of Vietnam was nothing less than a travesty and an incredible act of betrayal to the dedication and loyalty the war dogs gave our armed forces. I can only ask why our nation has failed to honor these patriotic and dedicated war heroes.

For the K-9 Corps and their memory, this is their story.

INTRODUCTION

None Came Home is the dramatic story of a young American G.I. who finds himself away from home for the first time in the faraway battlefields of Vietnam. Realizing his situation, he encounters a way to better his chances for survival. After a demonstration, the youth volunteers for duty in a very little known unit, the K-9 Corps, and is immediately paired with an equally inexperienced 13-month-old German shepherd named King.

We follow these two partners through their training, growth, and baptism of fire. The binding devotion and love that grows between this young man and his dog allow them to face the overwhelming odds and obstacles placed before them in their fight for survival and a return passage to the homes they once knew.

In a foreign country and climate, boy and dog must face the natural dangers and predators of the jungle terrain, the rainy monsoon season, sweltering heat, and what is considered by the leading military experts as the "world's most prolific jungle warfare fighting army on earth." Trust and loyalty was crucial, for the survival of both canine and human soldier. They depended on each other.

As the partnership matures, each soldier's promise to send the other home provides the foundation for a devotion that directs their course and provides the strength to overcome their fears and doubts.

This is their story.

Chapter I
RETURN TO SAIGON

"Let us be proud that by our bold, new initiatives, and by our steadfastness for peace with honor, we have made a breakthrough toward creating in the world what the world has not known before-a structure of peace that can, not merely for our time, but for generations to come."

Second Inaugural Address of President Richard M. Nixon:
Saturday, January 20, 1973

Three men: two white, one black. Wearing black berets and clandestine jungle camouflage fatigues, with no identification markings. They carry loaded backpacks and green duffel bags while running in unison through artillery shelling, machine-gun fire, and mortar explosions from uniformed and civilian-attired Asian men in trucks, tanks and automobiles. All hell has broken loose and chaos is the order of the day. Men cry while women and children scream. Ubiquitous smoke and fire hide the sun at mid-day in the muddy sky.

Pausing to catching their breath, no words are spoken. They look everywhere, not missing a thing as they hide from everyone. No friends or allies. They are alone, up-front where the action is. Well accustomed to it by now, they wouldn't have it any other way.

Their eyes squint to see an American helicopter taking off from the roof of a distant building. "The Embassy, we go this way," commands the first soldier. Instantaneously, they rise and, on the run, head for the smoke-blanketed noise of heavy mortar and gunfire.

Slipping around debris-laden alleyways and running through streets of carnage and mayhem, they finally reach the outskirts of the city and scramble through a mortar-shell destroyed wire perimeter fence. Minutes later, having breached the chaos and finding temporary refuge in the middle of a open pasture, the men sense a certain stillness among the desolate fields, but still scarred by remnants of partially destroyed buildings.

They know their destination well. As the soldiers cross the field their feet step on familiar concrete ground and they recognize their surroundings—the landing tarmac of an airbase. To their left and up the ridge they spot what they came for. "Hasn't changed much," one mumbles. The others agree.

They race up a small incline on a winding, muddy and dirt road and the men clear away branches and brush felled by the day's fighting. Now, cautiously,

1

they approach an old wooden field shed. They remember many a good beer and laugh shared in there, but now that seems like another lifetime.

Broken empty stalls and sandy pits stretch the length of the shack and a few empty collars with worn leashes line the walls amidst empty or half-filled water buckets—nothing but memories and ghosts from the not-too-distant past. "All deserted and yet, I can still hear them." A cold dark wind carries the ever-approaching night with smoke and the din of distant carnage.

Dropping their packs, they search the rest of the area for anybody or thing that may cause trouble or alarm, but a slow grin creases their faces as they approach the old deuce 1/2; a huge dusty behemoth of a truck made to go where no human being should want to. The colossal rhino, caked in mud and grease, would emerge from the jungles, determined to crash and break down any obstruction in its path. This dependable, now discarded relic was the testimony of a historic legacy—what was once Vietnam. "She was always a good truck. It's good to have her back again."

Suddenly, all three freeze like statues as the first signs of emotion escape their trembling bodies.

"There's the three crates! Oh, God!"

"Is that them?"

"It has to be. We can't stay much longer." They open the first one slowly, peek inside and smile.

"Nail it shut", the second man says.

"Getting dark, it's about that time. Let's move!"

With a gentle reverence, the three boxes are securely tied on the flatbed of the truck. Diligently, the men check the cargo ropes, which are fastened onto a loading plank, and secure the lifts to hold the precious freight in place. "Take it easy with that top box. That one's mine." They all smile.

Two of the soldiers, Dee and Luker, climb in the truck while the third, Pete, climbs on the back with the boxes. "Nice and smooth, fellas," he warns.

"Yeah, just like Pappy!" smiles Luker, jumping in the side door of the riding compartment.

"Jesus, Pappy," Dee sighs behind the wheel, "I wish he were here now. He drove these roads laughin', cursin' and hollarin' for more. There wasn't a hole or a bump in them he didn't like. Ha!"

Dee turns the key and the huge reliable truck belches a dark cloud of smoke, answering the crackling roar of its big diesel engine. In first gear, the screaming truck slowly moves toward the perimeter fence and the jungle road where they roll to a stop. They know worst is just ahead in the direction of the docks and the waiting ship that will take them to safety. Dee glances at Luker and watches his big black friend empty the huge duffel bag of its contents: two M-16 rifles, three.45 caliber handguns, and a case of grenades, which Luker arranges in an easily accessible place, knowing their value all too well. He hears Pete setting up the.50 cal. on its brackets atop the deuce's cabin. The sound of Pete loading and cocking the gun personifies the man's determination.

A smile crosses Dee's face as Pete fires off two bursts: the first for settings, second for range. It's the grin that acknowledges the destiny of these three men. This moment has already been written. It was whispered in the wind the instant the trio joined the special K-9 forces, and now that it was here there was no place he would rather be.

"What?" asks Luker?

"Nothing." Dee quips, "Besides, you wanna live forever?" That draws a smirk from Luke remembering the old battle cry from Dee's father's 1st. Division, Army, in the First World War.

"Besides," chimes in Pete, leaning through the rear window, "the people back in Washington ain't gonna be too happy about this!" Now, all three are smiling as Dee takes in a deep breath and looks kindly at his two faithful friends.

"Let's go home."

Suddenly, two shots explode from the jungle striking the oversized truck's reinforced grill. Small-arms gunfire sprays from the surrounding trees as darkness sweeps the area. Pete yells from the back, "Infantry regulars! They're all over the place and getting closer."

"The RVN troops are surrendering and switching sides," hollers Luker.

"Charlie was always Charlie," Dee adds, lighting a cigar and inhaling deeply as he contemplates the deteriorating situation. Something ol' Clint Eastwood would do, he muses. "Hey, remember that Clint movie we saw? Good, Bad and the Ugly? He always had great music to work with. Hey, Angel Eyes, I guess it's time now to play some of that music I know you brought."

Remembering an old debate they all once had about how great the different era's of music had represented the different attitudes of the nation, Luker fumbles around in the duffel bag and pulls out a tape. He slams it into the truck's tape deck as the big deuce jumps up into gear and rambles forward over the darkening jungle road.

"This oughta make them remember us and what it used to mean, when messin' with the United States meant something".

The pulsating bass and quick, gyrating rhythm now blares from the deuce's speakers. Satirically in sync with the heavy shooting, crashing, and driving mayhem, the homemade soundtrack raises everyone's awareness and spirits.

"YEEEEEHOWWWWWW!!! screams Pete from the top of his lungs.

A bullet pelts Luker's right forearm but he continues to shoot his M-16 and throw grenades at the surrounding trees and attempted roadblocks assembled by the Viet Cong soldiers. The shattered windshield finally crumbles but Dee, never lifting his foot, drives on over the half mud, half tarred roadway. He fires his M-16's 20-round clips into the darkness on auto bursts, biting down hard on his now unlit cigar. The deuce starts to spin then halts momentarily as it collides with a roadblock. Dee shoves the truck back into gear and the rampaging bull jumps again, leaving a shower of leaves, sand, dirt, debris and concrete in its wake.

At that moment however four VC leap onto the truck. Pete, wounded in the right leg and bouncing helplessly in the truck's bed, cannot stand but still manages to stab a VC with his side knife and knock off another trying to climb on board the back of the screaming truck. Luker turns and fires on the third man as he jumps Pete from the rear. Pete staggers, desperately attempting to stay inside the bouncing vehicle, but he's hit again by another shot from the third soldier's weapon. As both Pete and the soldier fall onto the boxes, he manages to hold onto the ropes as Luker fires again, killing Pete's attacker.

The fourth assailant swings around to the operator's side of the truck and stabs the side of Dee's left arm. With another thrust, he delivers a glancing blow off Dee's forearm and onto his chin. Dee, struggling to control the truck's wheel, grips the soldier in a vice-type headlock and, with his right hand, reaches for the pistol Luker had placed on the seat next to him. He fires point-blank into his attacker's face, and the man falls off the truck in a heap. The aged vehicle, seemingly knowing the importance of its cargo, recovers it's balance and gathers speed, leaving its pursuers in the dust.

"Just a little further, ol' girl," coaxes Dee.

Just ahead, the team spots more enemy soldiers on their way to the docking area. "We got to get past them," Luker hoarsely whispers to Dee.

Again, the enemy is everywhere as the truck bursts through the last roadblock, a hastily put together combination of old weathered Datsun trucks and cars. The deuce hits the sand dunes, and braces for its final leg.

"Are they there?" Pete asks.

"Does it matter? We're here, and we're not going anywhere else."

As the truck emerges from the jungle overgrowth and onto the beach, the world erupts behind them in a blinding fury of fire and explosions—something like a fireworks display back home on the fourth of July. This time, the show prevents enemy reinforcements from following them to their waiting ship. They see the old freighter at the dock about three hundred yards ahead with a full head of steam and smoke billowing from its stack. The fourth member of the team, Ike, and the Thai marines, who were left here to defend this improbable escape, furiously shooting the bush and surrounding terrain.

The marines have set up an outer perimeter line of fire, but from the truck, the three men can see that some spots have broken down into hand-to-hand fighting.

"Sak's men doin' a good job!" Pete shouts. "Those Thai Tiger commandos are some of the best fighters in the world."

"Yeah! I'm glad they're with us! I guess we owe him another bottle for this." The sheer numbers are, however, against the team as they start to retreat back toward the large freighter. Dee slams on the brakes, thundering to a stop at the dock. Peppered with bullet and shrapnel scars and ravaged tires, the aged and bloodied but unbowed truck has accomplished its last assignment. The wounded yet determined trio, along with four Thai soldiers, quickly lock the metal clamps on the ship's rusty crane to the rope-knots and, in one continuous heave, hoist the boxes with Pete sprawled on top, securing the ropes, onto a wooden skiff, over the side railing, and aboard the ship. That accomplished, the remaining Thai commandoes and Ike scurry on board the departing vessel. Out of time, Dee and Luker carry one another up the boarding ramp, collapsing on deck in a bloody clump as the wavering veteran freighter slowly pulls out of port.

Creaking and complaining every inch of the way, but now out of land-based gun range, the team finally takes a deep breath. The burning carnage left behind still lingers in the strained silence of the night air. Quickly reaching a full head of steam, the old freighter pressures its limits at 20 knots.

"Gun-boats! Three and closing fast!" shatters the night. Once again, small cannon fire and 50 caliber machine guns are tearing the helpless freighter apart.

"No!" Dee screams. "God dammit! We've come too far for this to happen."

"We've only got small ordinance and not enough of that!" yells Ike from the captain's office on the upper deck.

"Mayday...Mayday...Mayday," he repeats into the radio microphone, begging for a miracle.

"S.O.S., S.O.S...Please! Thai national freighter, with Americans on board, under attack by enemy gunboats. Please. Is there any help? Our coordinates are..."

A damaging shot rips a fatal tear in the ship's side. Wailing in pain, the vessel threatens to capsize.

"One more shot like that and it's over," cries the captain, his calls for more speed falling on deaf ears.

"S.O.S. Help us please! Is there anybody out there? S.O.S! S.O........."

Chapter II
THE CALL

1968: Lackland AFB, San Antonio, Texas

In the clear, characteristically hot Texas sun, a group of approximately 60 Air Force regulars in green fatigues march in columns of four toward an unfamiliar section of their massive training base. They march in unison, eyes straight ahead. Stepping smartly in cadence, they descend a small incline and approach a colorless one-story building.

"Column halt!" The Sgt. barks and the unit stops crisply. "At Ease!"

"What's up, sarge?" a voice asks.

"We're here to see a show," the detail's commander retorts.

"Smells bad over here, sarge. I think Collins here got *creative* over last night's ravioli."

"Your wife's ravioli, Gatto!"

"Cool it you clowns. You'll get used to it."

A tall man, also in fatigues but with four stripes on his sleeves, rounds the corner of the building and unlocks the fence.

"This way, men."

"Watch the mud."

"Go around and take a seat in the bench reviewing area." One by one, the soldiers pass through the wire fence and file into an arena lined with wooden benches about seven rows high. Grabbing seats next to buddies, the soldiers stare silently at a new group of soldiers marching sharply as they enter a large fenced ringed corral directly in front of them.

On the left side of each man, a dog strides in precise cadence, its shoulder blades directly aligned with the handler's left leg. The dogs do not pull, responding only to the actions of their human handlers. In single file, the men march to the center of the corral and execute a sharp right, never once losing step with the dogs. Their smart uniforms are crisp and creased with polished black boots and leggings tied "Paratrooper style." The well-groomed dogs, with confident strides and heads held high, *know* they look good. Silent stares radiate from the crowd as the men and dogs complete their entrance and face the stands in a single line.

If betting on a confrontation, a smart man would wager on the line of twenty men with their dogs over the many in the stands.

On command, all the men in line, except one handler in the center, turn smartly, slapping their left thighs. No words spoken to the dogs beside them.

The man in the center remains where he is, and the obedient dog by his side never flinches.

"Look at that dog. I don't think an earthquake could separate him from that guy."

"Now that's loyalty", says one of the recruits in the stands.

"My wife doesn't even do that," adds the newlywed Gatto.

"Yeah, I know," teases McNeal from the back, and the snickering carries out to the motionless man and his dog.

While the other men and their dogs assume positions at the far end of the arena, the singled-out soldier and his statuesque dog now begin their routine.

Calmly, the handler drops the leash in his right hand. Next, without looking at or touching the canine, he waves his left hand, palm flat, in front of the dog's face and across its nose. The man starts to walk, eight, nine, ten, eleven feet in front of the dog. Meanwhile, the animal never flinches, its eyes fixed intently on his partner. About 15 feet away, the soldier, still walking away, slaps his left thigh. Immediately the dog springs forward. In a few quick strides he catches up to the handler and rejoins him at his left leg, walking, now off-leash, in perfect cadence. Side by side, man and canine execute a crisp right turn and about-face. The demonstration of execution is a thing of classical beauty to watch. Again, the handler glides his left hand in front of the dog's face and immediately, his four-legged companion freezes as the man continues to walk. About 15 feet away, the soldier about-faces. Face to face with his dog, he slaps his left thigh and the canine springs forward again, approaches his master's right side, circles behind, and sits at the man's left thigh to face the stands once more.

A round of applause begins to generate, representing the stunned admiration of the troops. The spectators stare as the handler thoroughly pats and rubs his partner in deep praise. In turn, the eyes of the dog, glazed with affection and happiness, gaze adoringly at his handler. They walk off to the fence perimeter and another dog and handler assume center stage.

This man also drops his leash, walks about 15 feet away and about-faces while his dog sits attentively. The handler raises his right arm, then, lowers it forward to his thigh. Immediately, the canine drops to the ground on its stomach. The soldier, palm up, brings his arm to shoulder height, and the dog sits up straight. The handler swings his right forearm across his chest, the dog lunges forward, circles behind the man, and sits at his left side. No words were spoken between the man and his canine, yet the team shared a magnificent understanding. Amidst a crescendo of applause, the handler again affectionately praises his canine partner.

Now the remaining dogs and men, ready for their turn, begin running in step around the fenced arena. One by one, the canine teams break off in a straight line toward a series of obstacles. The first structure, a 7-foot high wall, the dogs clear effortlessly. Next, the dogs dig under a wire fence and enter a pipe-tunnel about

20 feet long. As the handlers run to the end of the structure, his dog's head magically emerges. The dogs climb up a stepladder and across a thin wooden platform. The dogs leap from the high apparatus to the ground, landing, as always, next to their handler's left thigh. Finally, the soldiers leash their dogs and assemble at the far end of the arena, concluding a magnificent demonstration of agility, confidence and teamwork.

Suddenly, an obvious change alters the temperament of the canines. Once playful, the animals are now all business. The handlers have straddled the dogs and replaced their metal choke collars with more supportive leather collars. As if someone switched on a red light, the transformed dogs have become statues of tightened muscles and keen attention while their handlers gently pat their heads and whisper words of praise and encouragement.

Now, another man, completely encased in protective padding, enters the venue. Apparently, the dogs were waiting for this guy. Straining at their leads on strong hind legs, front paws wildly reaching for the padded man, he slowly menacingly approaches the aroused canines.

At the signal, one handler drops his leash and his dog lunges forward. The canine, covering the near 50 feet in three running leaps and tears into the man, who protectively feeds the animal his padded left arm. This wisely prevents giving the dog the deciding factor on which area to attack. As the dog's handler hurriedly approaches, his partner's vicious assault has already ripped the covering and begun to tear the inner layer of protecting cushioning surrounding the "agitator".

"Out!" commands the handler, and immediately the dog releases the padded arm, which if not for the protective covering, would have already been reduced to a broken, bloody mess. Next, the handler orders the mock intruder to remain silent and motionless and instructs his dog, still off lead, to remain "alert" and cautions his partner to "watch him." A commanding silence permeates the corral as the young soldier approaches the cushioned captive. Meanwhile, the dog's total focus is on only one thing, his handler's enemy. As the handler reaches the mock antagonist, he lunges quickly for the handler, knocking him to the ground. Instantly, the dog launches, covering an incredible seven or eight feet, and ferociously gnaws the chest pads of the enemy. Without a doubt, a real enemy would have died immediately, if not for the protective padding.

Regaining himself, off the ground, the handler yells "out," and once again, the dog reluctantly releases the assailant. As the handler gathers the dog's leash, he lovingly praises his faithful four-legged companion and returns to the arena's fence to rejoin the other dogs and handlers. Now, the unit walks slowly, in single file, toward the exit gate and disappears behind the training area building.

When the last dog exits the arena, the padded man attempts to get up. Two assistants help him stand and start removing his pads. Gradually, the shape of a man emerges and waves to the crowd. As the audience applauds his willingness to be "sacrificed" to the dog, whispers of "who is he" circulate through the stands. Still sweating and out of breath, he removes the last of the protective cushions from his legs and approaches the bleachers.

"Hello, I'm Sergeant Causwell, and I'm one of the instructors here at Lackland AFB K-9 Training School", he says in a deep southern drawl.

"We all take turns being the agitator for the dogs to have some 'fun,' but on a hot day like this I'm gonna have to start pullin' some rank," he quips with a smile, looking in the direction of the other two younger staff instructors.

"I'm here today to ask for a few volunteers. I won't bullshit you guys. I know who you are. Right out of basic and into your job training as Security Policemen. You've just recently been given orders for overseas, Southeast Asia to be exact, if I'm not mistaken. The last few months of intense training and placement probably got you a "knot" in your ass, already. That's all right. It would get most everyone in your situation, but I figure this is the best time to come to you because we only want the ones that can still function and make decisions at a time like this. It's the guys under extreme pressure who can still look around and want more I'm talking to now. I'm betting there are a few of you in this group. We're also getting mighty close to the big show and it's you guys that would make up a big part of it.

I won't kid you. Up to recently our guys were getting their ass kicked over there. 'Charlie' pretty much had his way in when, where and how this little fracas was going to be fought and all we've been doing was reactionary mop-up. The first couple years of our involvement in Vietnam, they lived and hid in the jungle, the country's natural geography, and with years to perfect their tactics and planning, came and went without a second thought. They lived in and off the land and using the cover of night, they mortar and infiltrate our installations at will, laying booby-traps and singling out strategic targets. In short—producing big moral and logistic problems for us. But now, K-9 has been invited to this dance and we're headed for our biggest challenge, yet. We're going over there to stop all this crap and take on the vaunted Viet Cong on their own turf."

The seated men swapped hesitant looks. "March of this year a task force of 315 dogs and their handlers shipped out to Southeast Asia and Vietnam. This is the first concentrated build-up in the three years since K-9 was formally introduced as Project Top Dog back in '65. Up 'till now, we've been just getting the program organized and to see it's effectiveness. But, now we're in, "full hog" It is a historic occasion to be sure, for it makes this conflict 'official.' K-9 has been a driving, integral force in every major skirmish this country has ever experienced. Our dogs have excelled in battles for this nation since we've been fighting the British and it would be almost sacrilegious if K-9 weren't invited to this party, too! Just last week, the second detachment of more than 325 K-9 teams left for deployment and now we're setting up the last detachment for September. We thought a few of you guys might want to come along".

"Let me tell you, canines have gone to war with man since the Stone Age. For God's sake, cave paintings have dogs fighting along side, men against the dinosaurs. The Romans used the dog's keen sense of smell and hearing to alert them of approaching enemies and charge their front lines.

Estimates, today, say using the dog's natural instincts at night equates one dog and handler to seven armed men. We have heroic dogs from all the wars our country has fought and scores of stories about dogs that saved whole units from annihilation during battle. I'm sure you've all seen Rin Tin Tin save Rusty's little ass every week on TV, but that really can happen. This here is a partner you won't ever have to worry about keepin' your back if shit hits the fan. He won't leave you, and you know what? You won't leave him, neither. A handler and his dog is a superb fighting force, a majestic melting of two into one. Did you see those teams a few minutes ago? They were all green recruits a few weeks ago, just the same as you are now. Right now they're ready to face the unknown together, and they're ready to confront the Fires of Hell, together, if necessary.

Where we're going no one is going to like you, but you'll be the most respected and requested man, there. Just by the nature of the job you're doing. Did I mention that the enemy has put "bounties" out on us, over there? And, here's one of the reasons. When you got a 100-pound flashing fury running at you at 47 m.p.h. and all you can do is hear it getting closer to you without you seeing it and you got no place to hide, you have two choices, my friend. You either shit or you go blind, and it still doesn't help. And gentlemen, here's the best part. In Charlie's religion, it's the cat and the elephant that are the holy animals. Dogs are devils and they're deathly afraid of 'em! They know we're going to take all their advantages they had up 'til now away from them. They won't be able to run and they certainly won't be able to hide from us anymore, either.

"I told you guys before, I won't bullshit you. There's a job that going to get done and it's going to take men with heads on their shoulders and hearts in their chests. Let the dog be your eyes, ears, legs and nose. If you want to make a difference, be proud and join a little known, very elite force that never disappoints. Come join us.

I'm passing out a little story about a K-9 team, and I would like you to read it. Then, if you have any questions or are interested in joining us, fill out the back of this page and get it back to me by Friday. That gives you three days. Our next class begins Monday. Oh, and don't be too surprised to see some Navy and Marine dudes mixing in. At the present time there's only three K-9 facilities in the world: one in Japan, one in Germany, and ours here at Lackland. That's why we take only the men who want to join this elite tradition, the tradition of the War Dogs."

*   *   *

On the way back to the barracks, the usual bantering and kidding was absent. The private K-9 demonstration really impacted the men, and a lot were seriously mulling over the invitation. Throughout lunch the conversation centered on the dogs and the subsequent realities of actually volunteering. Of course, there was the guy who already made up his mind "never to volunteer" for anything. Then you had others who were just too damn cautious to get all worked up over something this "involved."

After the Sergeant's little pitch, we were shown the dog kennels and met the handlers that had performed the demonstration. They were real nice guys and genuinely enthusiastic about K-9. I preferred their spirit to the typical stream of constant complaints. One of the handlers, Bobby, said he was just like us a few weeks ago, but now he had a purpose. He really loved his dog, Ronn, and was very confident and proud of their advancement and training. He had just received his overseas orders too and, after a demo, decided to go with K-9. "If I had the choice of facing Charlie either with a gun, or a dog and a gun," he said, "I'd take the dog even without the gun." As for my personal decision, passing through the K-9 Hall of Fame clinched it.

On the walls of the K-9 Hall of Fame hung pictures of some of the finest looking dogs one will ever see. A few dogs stood out, like Stubby, York, and Chips. Stubby was a World War I dog. He wore a blanket-like drape covered with medals. His awards were the medals of soldiers that Stubby's actions had saved. Chips, who fought in World War II and saved his entire platoon in France from an Italian machine gun nest, And, York is credited with not losing a single man during his stint of 154 combat patrol mission in Korea, from either booby-trap or ambush. There was already talk about a dog named Nemo from our Vietnam conflict. According to the stories, he saved a whole group of guys and alerted to enemy infiltrators trying to blow up the big Tan Son Nhut Air Base, in Saigon.

Bobby wanted us to meet his dog. Beaming with genuine pride as we approached his dog's stall, the other canines started barking and jeering at us through the kennel doors. One of the guys told me to open the door but I wasn't even thinking about going there. Ronn jumped up and, wagging his tail, immediately found Bobby in the middle of the crowd. Ronn's bark was now one of welcome for his master. Then Ronn starting barking at the other dogs, probably saying "Shut-up, this is my guy." I watched all of this intently, and some of the other dogs actually stopped barking. Thoroughly impressed, I was seriously leaning toward K-9. Though the gate separated Bobby and Ronn, they were in each other's arms and nothing could divide them.

Bobby told us the dogs were all born and bred Americans, and were mostly house pets donated by families from across the country. When they started, they were very green. But, after their entry testing and physicals, all the dogs are trained by their handler, who are first instructed by the Lackland training staff.

"What are these empty runs for, Bobby?" one of us asks.

"Those are for your dogs when they arrive in a couple weeks."

Back at lunch, the guys joked about what some of the dogs must have thought when they first laid eyes on their handlers. We were told there had to be a mutual "meeting of the minds" as to who was gonna "run" the team.

"So, are you gonna volunteer?" one of my buddies asked.

I wanted to say yes, but, being cautious, I said I wanted to read the pamphlet first. "I might go with it," I added. Much to my surprise, Wayne Luker, a good guy from Philly with a lot of street-smarts and savvy, the one that was "too cool" to ever volunteer for anything, said he liked the idea too. Looking at each other for the first time, we suddenly saw a common fit between us. I guess K-9 was already living up to its hype about "a close, elite, little known family."

That night, after reading the pamphlet, I sent out my registration slip and lay on my bunk trying to figure out how I was going to tell my parents. I must admit I've got great parents. Sometimes they would try to change my mind about a lot of things, but they already know they won't. Time and again, they wind up having to giving me the encouragement and support to carry out impossible tasks I had no right to start in the first place. But this one felt so right. This time I didn't worry about making a mistake. Just whether or not I'd be accepted.

The next few days crawled, and talk about the dogs dwindled away. On Saturday, a card game broke out against regulations. I'll never forget ol' Parker's face when the barracks officer, making rounds, caught him drinking a beer and holding the deck of cards. It was funny as hell. What was this asshole going to do? Ship Parker to Vietnam? The gang booed as the officer led Parker out in handcuffs and cheered when he later released him. Apparently, the Captain had a little more discretion and had a "discussion" with the dopey Lieutenant. A little common sense certainly would have gone a long way. Anyway, Parker became a hero and we all headed to the "canteen" for a 3.2 beer binge.

Chapter III
WELCOME

Monday morning finally arrived and I went to breakfast. Following Sunday's bulletin ordering "all men who sent in K-9 registrations to report to the kennels after breakfast," I walked past the barracks and headed slowly toward the shed where we had seen the demonstration five days before. Looking around, I realized no one else was coming with me. "Oh God," I thought, "Am I the only asshole?"

However, as I reached the crest of the hill overlooking the kennel, I saw about twenty other guys waiting outside the hut. Feeling much better, I approached the group. Luker saw me and came over to slap me five. "O.K., New York's here. I guess we're cool now."

A few minutes later, a green canvassed beast of a truck, in dire need of a wash, rumbled up to the shed and roared to a stop, spraying dirt and dust from its thick, virtually bullet-proof all-terrain tires. As the back of the canvas swung open, men in green fatigues jumped from the vehicle in "twos". The men wore signatures of various company units and were of different rank. I recognized a couple of sergeants and corporals, but the Navy "dudes" decals I didn't know. A handful of rattled Marines, relieved to escape the truck, immediately straightened up. I then laid eyes on the world's cantankerous soldier. The strange, disheveled guy was laughing and talking to himself, muttering something about "drivin' too slow." A three striper in the Air Force, "Buck" Sgt. "Pappy," ambled out of the driver's seat of the still rattling protesting monster truck.

"Sounds like the ol' deuce needs a tune-up there, Pappy, smiled tech Sgt. Causwell, knowingly.

"Never you mind, and leave the "deuce½" alone. She wouldn't know what to do if you gave her a tune-up or a bath," the driver snarled.

"So, we're all here!" shouted T/Sgt. as he opened the shed door.

"Thanks, but I already knew that," said Tech Sgt. Langley, a five-striper, as he emerging from building.

Pappy, I swear, was a true "side-kick", a character, straight from the movies, without a script. The kind that you could always depend on and a man you'd want to have in a tight spot. He is the genuine article, and was probably well on his way long before there even was even a "Walter Brennen" or "Wallace Berry" character created. Too much a veteran to be just a three-striper, he must have seen one too many "situations", in his day. His presence could break up a High Mass on Sunday, but I had a feeling he would come in handy where we were going. Scratching his head and mumbling to himself, he fell in with the rest of us as we stood at attention for Tech.

"Welcome gentlemen. Welcome and thank you for answering our call. You're all gonna be pleasantly surprised by this detail. This will live up to all its hype and billing. If you guys want action and adventure, you got it! We can't and won't pull any punches here because we just don't have the time for it. You're going to do this and be the best, or you go back where you came from. It's that simple. We'll assist in any way we can, but everything you're gonna need is already in you, or you're out. Many lives, including your own, will depend on it. We don't bullshit here. We can't afford to. We expect and demand the same from you. We show you *once* and we want to see it from you, or a real close *inventive* variation of it that produces the same result.

All of you who make it through training and are still here in eight weeks will get a two-week leave to go home or to do whatever. Then you'll reassemble back here for a trip into history. You will be a part of the third and final leg of the biggest airlift of war dogs ever undertaken by The United States. You will all be deployed immediately into areas desperately begging for and needing our services.

So here we are. I will be interviewing all the men I haven't yet. In the meantime, the other instructors are here to introduce themselves and show you around the place. Ask them questions and get comfortable. This will be your last chance to do that for a while. In our training, free time is wasted time. I highly recommend you initiate a physical regimen for yourself because when the dogs come in you not only have to keep up with them, but you gotta lead and be able to stop and direct them. Here, we run wherever we go and we're in the best physical shape we can be. Now let's get these interviews over with and start being Dog Men."

Proceeding alphabetically, I was finally called after about 45 minutes. I watched everyone's face as they emerged from the shed and headed toward the rest of the group at the dogs' training and obstacle course. A few laughs filtered through the low conversation and serious attention. I wanted this. I wanted to belong to this force.

I remembered my father's pictures as a New York City fireman. In my memory, he was always with the company mascot, Smokey. I remember one photo, my father lying seriously injured on the ground in front of a burning building while Smokey leaned over his helmet, comforting him. Dogs do that and I wanted that kind of a partner for my cover.

I entered the room. The Tech was sitting at his desk. "John, welcome! I read your records and your registration. You no doubt qualify educationally, and I'm glad to have a guy with your background here."

"I don't understand," I said, surprised.

"That's exactly my point! You don't know shit about K-9 or what you're doing here, but you know that and aren't afraid to try. It's the guys who think they know dogs that give me a problem. You, I can form and shape along with your dog."

I was afraid to say yes, but I did understand his logic. I just smiled and he smiled back. "You're going to be a fine dog handler," he said, nodding his head. "You'll make K-9 proud, son. I know it. Now, *you* got to know it. We'll just keep doing it until you feel comfortable with it. Do you have any further questions? Don't worry. They'll all be answered sooner or later in the next few weeks. We'll have one more meeting like this to evaluate your real work before you get your dog. Work hard and keep an open mind." He shook my hand and told me to rejoin the others. "We've all some work to do for the next couple of weeks."

Just like that. I walked in the office nervous and uncertain, and walked out a confident and energized man, raring to go after only a pat on the back and a few words of encouragement. Interesting, sort of like what the handout said about training the dogs—"repetition and praise."

The other guys were talking with three of the staff trainers as I joined them. Turns out Bobby, his dog Ronn, and the other guys who performed the demo were shipped out over the weekend to installations around the country for some practical experience in the field. They would rejoin us and the other dog-handlers when the time came to go to Southeast Asia. Rumor has it that ours will be the largest employment yet. "Operation Pipeline" will be completed by then. I now pray we will be ready for it.

The following two weeks were devoted to classroom studies. We had to know what we were doing and how to do it before we met our dogs. In the meantime, the guys got to know each other fairly well. A few of us had been together since basic training, which felt like a lifetime ago. The other recruits proved to be good guys too, although we had the usual tag-fest that always exists when different forces or units merge, but surprisingly, the transition went pretty smooth.

That, we learned, is what K-9 is. A brotherhood, consisting of all the military branches, together, that must always be able to operate cohesively anywhere to perform a variety of functions. First, K-9 executes the basic functions of security/sentry work, which involves mainly perimeter patrolling outside the fence and surrounding area of a base or installation. Then, the force takes responsibility for securing highly important designated areas against infiltration, thievery, or sabotage. K-9 also performs crowd control in specified areas and entry locations, and now there was talk about using the dogs' superior sense of smell to detect drugs and explosives. While patrolling, the dogs were already used to detect enemies and booby-traps, and their success in saving lives in the field was highly understood.

In other wars, K-9 was used sparingly. The dogs mainly transported messages between commands, guarding prisoners, or located wounded and lost soldiers on the battlefield. K-9 never was given the opportunity to truly show their complete worth. However, times progress and job circumstances change. K-9 has met every test and has never failed. In the face of modern technology, the need for K-9 assistance has proven to continue in emergency situations.

"Repetition and praise." The dogs will respond with "repetition and praise." These two words now become ingrained in our lives, serving as a model for our own living—two words that will remain with us for the rest of our lives.

We are growing mighty fidgety for the final evaluation, but before we meet the dogs, we still needed to understand the special equipment, its function and care, and our job requirements. We also spend an awful lot of time exercising in the field.

The recruits are taught that K-9 works primarily at night. This heightens the advantage of the dogs' natural abilities: smell, sight, and hearing. We also learned a variety of safeguards for our own protection, like just how far a lighted cigarette can be detected, how to utilize the wind for smell, how one's eyes can adjust to the dark, and how to cover up one's presence in the field. We're taught to "walk where the dog walks", and "stop when the dog stops". Pay close attention to the dog's habits and movements. "He's communicating to you and he will save your life and all the men behind you, if you listen". We also receive plastic covers for our dog tags to muffle their "clanging" sound and stitched or crayoned out our uniform decals to black, so they won't give away our positions at night. Utilizing the cover of darkness is imperative to our job and our safety. I don't smoke but a lot of the guys were having trouble curtailing the habit. I wonder if that will be a problem later.

Finally, the training and direction concluded. The moment that we'd all been waiting for will arrive the next day. No one could sleep. At around 10 p.m., a first truck passed the barracks, heading toward the kennels, then another, then one more. Approximately six trucks stopped, unloaded, and left. A few guys wanted to steal down to the kennels and check out the movement, but with evaluations the next morning, they decided it wasn't such a brilliant idea. We were all giddy with excitement. Electricity charged the air, and sleep was the last thing on everyone's mind. The jokes and insults were flying faster and funnier than ever, but not a single fight erupted! While everyone was attacking, no one was the target. Everyone was united, and it was a good feeling.

A warm and sunny Monday arrived, and everyone was willingly up long before the wakeup call. Nobody wanted to screw up the final determining evaluation. The possibility of such heartbreak now was no joking matter. Over the past few weeks, the instructors had stressed that we shouldn't get too attached to our assigned canines. Then the instructor would share a story about a dog he once had. "Sure, he wasn't too attached."

It was 8:30A.M. Someone suggested we do the dogs' obstacle course ourselves, when the Tech entered. We could already hear the dogs in the back kennels barking like hell, and I wondered what they were thinking.

"When I call your name go over to that table and Sergeant Diaz will assign you a card. On that card will be your dog's name, I.D. number. Where?" he commanded.

"On the inside of the left ear Sergeant," we all answered in unison.

"And kennel stall number," he continued. "Then, I want you to meet your dog and start making friends. All other questions and information will be supplied this afternoon. They haven't been fed yet, which you can do after contact has been made and you're satisfied with the response. Remember; do not engage unless invited. We don't want any injuries. Clean out his stall with the hose if necessary, and give your dog fresh water. He'll be watching you, and so will we."

Chapter IV
KING

Luker and I looked at each other and laughed.

"That's it? Where's the evaluation? Maybe they forgot." Luker said. "You wanna go remind them?"

"Maybe we missed something," Parker suggested.

"Ah shit, Parker!" I said, "I didn't miss anything, did you?"

The four sergeant instructors and the tech were talking together, comparing reports. Presently, the tech approached us, indicating he wanted our attention. Everyone shut up but the dogs were still barking like hell. Grinning, the tech began. "This is the scoop on the evaluations. As it turns out, we got 26 dogs last night, and we've got 26 handlers. Nobody has clearly established himself as a natural-born dog handler, but nobody screwed up badly enough that the staff wanted to fire any of you, either. So, listen up you handlers, go to your dogs and lets get some K-9 in your blood."

A massive cheer erupted as the men hugged and congratulated one another. Even the staff joined in. It felt good to be a part of this small "family". Now, we turned our attention to the dogs. I can't remember what I was told when they called my name and gave me my card. I felt a pat on my back from Luker, but I was not touching ground as I approached the table. One of the instructors shook my hand and gave me a small index card: KING-4lM3-stall No. 27.

I thought of where he'd come from and where my life had been. Now we were about to meet. Was this my dog of destiny? Is this how it was supposed to be? Suppose one of us had been just a fraction of a second late? Would it have thrown off the entire situation? Slowly, with deliberate steps, I entered the kennels. As I passed the stalls, I congratulated the other handlers already talking to their assigned canines. I walked all the way to the back and took my first look at King-4lM3. He was beautiful, a genuine German Shepherd with classic black and tan markings, and as he stood in his stall looking me directly in the eye, I knew there had been no mistake.

He was a big dog, an unkempt canine, starved of personal attention and looking for a friend. Wagging his tail as I approached, King rose on his hind legs when I reached his kennel. He easily could have rested his front paws on my shoulders if not for the stall's gate. There we stood, gazing into one another's eyes, yet despite the humorous appearance we were intently sizing one another up. Yes, I could actually see it. He was smart and he would be friendly, but I could feel his spirit and sensed he'd bust my chops whenever he could. I loved him immediately.

First, I cleaned his stall and poured some fresh cool water. I started to talk to him while he drank but then stopped, wanting simply to observe my new friend and study all his special characteristics and actions.

Looking around, I noticed that no one had entered the stalls yet, but judging King, I sensed he was friendly enough to allow me to enter. I stood up and unlocked the kennel door. Instantly, his personality changed as he retreated to the rear of his pen. Reassuring him with my voice, I slowly began to open the gate, drawing a growl from the corner. "Ok big fella, it's your house," I said, closing the gate. Immediately, the play attitude resumed as he returned to the gate, tail wagging. I wasn't frightened or even disappointed, but rather impressed and respectful of this animal's individuality and insightful spirit. King's friendship would have to be earned.

Little did I realize that Sgt. Langley had witnessed the entire incident, and he approached me as I left the kennel. By the time I left King, he had allowed me to reach though the doorway and pet him.

"You got some dog there. He's special and it's written all over him. The name fits the personality. His coat is his spirit and his pride and you don't want to break it. Build it up and work with it. In the Navy, he's the flagship, and you have a tremendous responsibility to preserve that strength. He'd be no good, to you or himself, if he were overwhelmed or untrusting. If you feed and direct his spirit, he'll go anywhere and do anything for you. That's a tremendous dog."

I just stood there with so many feelings welling up inside that I thought I was going to burst.

I didn't want to break for lunch, but I went with the rest of the guys anyway and listened to their giddy laughter and stories. I grabbed two extra pieces of bread and some jelly for King. Maybe it would help loosen him up a little. I wanted desperately to fasten a collar on him and take him out of the stall by afternoon. He was very disheveled from lack of attention and I was convinced a decent grooming would improve his spirits.

When I returned to the stalls, King was waiting for me, standing on his strong hind legs to keep watch over the dividers. When he spotted me he jumped down to wait near the gate and as I began talking, he gradually, studying my every move, began to approach the wire screen that separated us. Everything we had discussed during our two-week classroom study was now enacted with amazing accuracy. King played the role of Hamlet and I well I really did wonder what he thought of me.

I reached into my bag, ripped off a piece of bread with jelly, and slid it under the door. As I had hoped, King studied it for a second, gave it a sniff then he gobbled it up. Nearing the door, he jumped up to place two massive front paws directly in front of me. I tore off another piece and offered it to him through the door. He accepted, carefully avoiding my fingers, and I must admit, I was swept with achievement. I talked to him a little more and he seemed to feel more at ease. It was then I made my decision.

Standing straight up, I unlocked his gate. Again, he immediately retreated to the back of the stall. As I opened the door he growled, but this time the wary rumble was not nearly as threatening, or so I thought. At that point, I was all the way in his domain, and if he really wanted to, he wouldn't have needed any more bread and jelly for a long time. It was a moment for the ages, I thought. However, sensing I could win King over, I knelt and placed my offering, the last piece of bread and jelly, by the kennel door. Ever so slowly King swallowed his threatening growl and approached, but he was still prepared for anything. His legs were visibly tightened, ready to spring, while his chest swelled with quantities of air large enough to fuel a sudden battle. While his glaring eyes had softened slightly, the majestic head remained cocked and guarded for the slightest threatening gesture, but I merely knelt and smiled, rambling encouragements as softly as possible. In our consciousness, we were the only two living beings.

Compromising, I pushed the bread, which was about five inches in front of me, a little further from my body, and that was the signal. King made his move, moving just close enough to grab the morsel. I in turn, slowly moved to smoothly uncap my canteen and gulp some cool water.

Suddenly, I had a brainstorm. Removing the metal cup fastened to the bottom of the canteen, I poured some water for King and placed the offering in the vicinity of the bread, just a bit closer to me this time. Just as I'd hoped, King began to drink. I was thrilled as I watched the dog's body relax. Yearning to jump and holler, I was restrained by visions of a startled dog ripping me apart. As I stood, King stopped drinking to stare at me.

His wagging tail diminished any threat, and I deliberately advanced toward my dog and stroked his large magnificent head for the first time.

The day's conclusion was well met, and as I met up with Luker, the dogs completely dominated our evening conversation. One or two guys had still not entered their dogs' areas. That had to be accomplished tomorrow. As for me, I was already contemplating giving King a bath.

Chapter V
TRAINING

As promised, I skipped breakfast and arrived at the kennel early. King badly needed a bath. His coat, urine-moistened and matted with dead hair, served as a magnet for dirt. Now that King was my partner, I wanted to improve his appearance.

That morning when I greeted him, he was wide-eyed and wagging his tail. I hosed out his stall and gave him some fresh water, constantly talking and reassuring him as I cleaned, but though he allowed me to enter and exit his stall, this would be the first time I planned on taking him out his kennel. Consequently, I was well prepared.

The leather attachment on my canteen belt, which now carried King's water cup, allowed me to hook all of the dog's equipment together: a specially-rolled chain or 'choke collar,' a leather 'working collar,' a muzzle, a 6-foot 'control' leash, and a 20-foot 'obedience' leash. The importance of the past two weeks of classroom instruction was instantly apparent.

First, I unhooked the choke collar and slipped it over King's head, but his massive shoulders allowed the collar to slide only part way down his neck. If not placed correctly the collar's choking effect would be nullified. To properly utilize the collar, one must allow the chain to slip through the larger ring on one end until the smaller ring on the opposite end stops the movement. This technique allowed the collar to rest loosely if the dog walked correctly but permitted the handler to discipline the dog by tightening or 'choking' the collar if his canine broke from the expected walking procedure.

After positioning the collar, I placed King in a sit. To do so, I attached the short, 6-foot control leash to his collar and shifted King to my left side. Holding the leash close and high, in my right hand, I pushed down, with my left, on King's rump while commanding him to "sit." The correlation of movement and command directed the dog's actions while teaching him to recognize the order. After correctly completing the exercise, I praised King. "Good boy," I enthused energetically as King sat, still unaware of his good behavior.

It looked well while it lasted and I smiled, but when I praised King he stood immediately. "No," I responded forcefully, returning his body to a sitting position beside my left leg. Again he attempted to rise. "No," I repeated, placing my left hand on his hindquarters and pushing down. "Sit. Stay." It took a few attempts, but I sensed King would be a fast learner.

As he sat, I straddled his body and hooked the muzzle to his face. This time he didn't budge. "Good boy," I crooned enthusiastically, rubbing his side. King enjoyed the praise, raising his head higher and higher with each compliment.

As a safety precaution, muzzles were equipped on the canines before they associated with other dogs and handlers. "Sorry," I said to King, "but it has to be done. You'll get used to it." A few seconds later, he struggled to take it off. "No," I said. King walked a few paces and attempted to remove it again. Eventually, as he repeated his struggles and I repeated my commands, he left the muzzle alone. Compromising, I managed to loosen it a bit.

Next, I led King outside to meet Luker and some other guys with their dogs.

Let's just say we did ok and I accomplished my goal—getting King (and myself) wet and soapy. Then I dried him, which he thoroughly enjoyed, and started to groom his coat, first with a steel comb worked against the grain, followed by a bristle brush to recover the coat's luster. I could tell he felt better, and after a few hours we rested on the grandstand with Luker and his dog, Diablo. A big, beautiful white, gray, and black Husky, Diablo got along with King quite well.

Together, we compared the rest of the recruits' dogs. Some were prepared to tear one another apart. Others stood alone, ignoring everyone. King and Diablo sat regally side by side as they inspected the other canines, and both Luker and I noted that we had partnered with two mighty fine animals.

I knew after some additional grooming, King would look terrific. He was a natural, sitting calmly on strong, thick legs with his head in the air and chest extended. And, as his tan and black coat began to glisten, in the sun, my pride swelled immeasurably.

That afternoon, after lunch and a change of clothes, the instructors told us where our canines were from and offered background specifications. At that point, I knew King and I were no accident. He hailed from Staten Island, New York, my hometown. "No way," the Sgt yelled, "we can't let these two foul-ups stick together! We've gotta break this up." I couldn't believe it. We were both raised in the City, and the Sarge was ranting about "two screw-ups!"

Luker was cracking up behind me and slapped me five. His dog, Diablo, came from Houston, Texas. "Big-city enough," he said.

We received the dogs' profiles and were advised to look up the addresses of the donating families and write them about their dogs and ourselves. Not only did I write but also I promised to visit King's family during my next leave so I could meet them personally and bring some pictures.

King's file stated that he was only 1-year-old, stood 56 inches, and should weigh in at around 98 pounds. King was a medium-large dog now and should grow somewhat bigger throughout the coming year.

Immediately, I paid a visit to my 'home-town' buddy and took him to the training area. The facility had a scale and I wanted to weigh him. All morning, during his bath, I'd felt nothing but ribs and I wanted to straighten that out now. Sure enough, King was a full eight pounds under.

"We'll fix that boy," I assured him as we jogged around the area, together.

The following day was the beginning of our last six weeks of training. Each period had a designated training expertise to cover. The first two weeks taught the ten basic commands a dog must learn for movement, containment and encouragement. All the commands should be spoken in a clear and commanding, unhesitant tone except for when praise is indicated.

1. "Stay"—spoken while handler places his left hand, palm in, in front of the canine's face to order it to halt.
2. "Heel"—spoken while slapping one's left thigh; the dog should remain by the handler's left side.
3. "No"-the command spoken in a harsh tone and a sharp jerk on the leash to tell one's dog it's not behaving correctly.
4. "Good Boy"—the command, spoken in an enthusiastic higher voice, while patting the dog's side for praise and to reward it for responding to an order correctly.
5. Down—the command and lowering of one's right hand, palm in, in front of the dog's face.
6. Up—the command and the raising of one's right hand, palm up; executed initially at a distance of approximately 5 feet, then gradually increased to distance desired.
7. Stop—the command and the holding of one's right hand outright, palm facing the dog; executed at increasing distances.
9. Come—the command and the movement of one's right hand, palm in, across one's chest; hold hand in place momentarily.
10. Out—the command to stop attacking a perpetrator or to release him at the handler's signal.

Initially, both hand signals and voice commands were utilized, but the voice instructions were gradually weeded out until the canines responded to hand signals only. We were told this would be very necessary when "in the field".

King didn't have a problem absorbing his training. I sometimes made mistakes, but King caught on quickly and really took to his activities, including the exercise area, without a problem. Every time he ran through the obstacle and exercise courses, he challenged me. Who could work faster, his actions seemed, him or me? I began to realize that King was actually whipping me in shape just to keep up with him. Many a time, I was the one huffing and puffing at the end of a course. He was rounding out us both into magnificent shape and I wanted him to be as proud of me as I was of him. It was often King who gave me the encouragement and determination to get the job done, as we both found ourselves accomplishing things we'd never dreamed, we constantly opted for more.

The best part, however, were the moments we rested, usually by ourselves in the shade of a tree. I would sit against the trunk and he would lie down beside me, his head resting on my stomach. Patting his forehead and talking to him, I'd read my mail. King would never interrupt. He appeared to understand the news from New York City.

It felt that we both recognized the great unknown we'd face in the near future, but we'd be ok as long as we were together. After all, we were hometown buddies.

With only four weeks of training left, time was flying. Luker and I, feeling increasingly uptight, decided to go into town and see the sights. The Alamo and the World's Fair were cool, and at night we hit a couple of discothèques for some music. San Antonio was a rocking town during The Hemisphere days of the '68 World's Fair. However, the only thing we talked about was the dogs; Luker feeling every bit for his Diablo that I felt for King.

By this time, the first six weeks of training were in the bank and now, the company was to leave the friendly confines of training school to meet the natural environs of actual working conditions. K-9 always works alone in isolated surroundings to take full advantage of the dogs' natural endowments: smell, hearing, and sight. Too much distraction and the animals were rendered useless. Ideally, K-9 worked in conjunction with the military's backup, but in most situations, the force served as a handler and dog unit on the front lines, ALONE.

Therefore, unless a trusting bond between dog and handler was achieved during the course of training, it was useless to continue. Through obedience, the mastering of commands, and indispensable private time, man and dog melded a team of understanding, loyalty and trust that nothing must break. If the unity was dismantled, both were destined for failure. In fact, we had to know each other so completely, that each could detect the slightest behavior change in the other. During the last two weeks outside of Lackland at Camp Bullis, in the highly isolated country setting, we'd face our final test and initiation.

To begin this highly critical phase, we participated in a going away ceremony to commemorate the completion of our Lackland training phase. The staff and all interested personnel were invited to review the recruits and the dogs before they began the job. This service was a time-honored military tradition before one left a station or embarked to new destination. We looked sharp in our finest fatigues and polished boots, and as we approached the kennels, the dogs barked just a little louder than usual. They knew something out of the ordinary was happening.

The day before, I groomed King to guarantee he'd look his best. He was growing and filling out now. No more ribs, just intense muscle and clear, bright eyes. My admiration for him was mirrored in his action towards me when we were together. Even some of the other handlers and staff had remarked on how "natural" our relationship was. There was no hesitancy or mystique between King and I. We knew we'd be there for each other.

As we paraded over the grounds I remembered a time, not too long ago, when I sat in the stands as a spectator. Now, I was the show. We demonstrated the dogs' skills and obedience with the obstacle course. The canines never disappointed. I found myself surprised and impressed by the advancement we'd achieved. Having gone through the paces, we assembled in a single line to face the reviewing stand and absorb the applause of the spectators. As Luker and I attempted to contain our giggles, I think I even saw King and 'Blo slap five.

Then, I heard a ruffle of giggles and laughter filter from the stands. That certainly wasn't in the program and I quickly looked to see what was happening. Instantly, my mouth dropped at the most amazing thing I ever saw. Of the six dogs in line, one had broken his sitting position, raised his hind leg, and started urinating on his handler's leg! In the history of the program, I don't think such a thing had ever happened. The staff didn't even know how to respond.

The handler remained at attention as the dog finished and sat down again. With that, the reviewing stand broke out again in applause and mock encouragement for the embarrassed handler, or was it for the dog? Immediately, I looked down at King. With his head turned in the direction of the incident, I knew he'd seen it all. He never missed a thing, I mused. He looked up at me, and his eyes revealed only one thing. "Don't even think about it," I shot back with a glare of my own. He instantly looked away, but I caught his eyes peeking once more to quickly examine mine. Yes, I was still watching him. He still had a little "whimsy", in him, and I could never let him catch me laughing at a stunt like that.

When we returned to the kennel, we heard Sgt. Diaz screaming "crazy Spanish" at the handler. We were laughing hysterically, but poor Diaz, he was out of his mind. We found out later that the handler arrived at the kennels late and hadn't taken his dog out for his routine, so the dog just said, "piss on it!"

Fortunately, the stunt did break the tension that had mounted prior to the last phase of our training. Two weeks left and the guys were still feeling their individual accomplishments. We had two more tasks to complete—the aggression and night patrol segments. The time had come to find out if a dog had it in him to perform his main task of protection—alert and containment.

Many dogs fail this section due to their temperament and nature. Now, it was up to me to shift King's relatively good temperament from play to nasty and aggressive killer instincts. No more house-pet days for these dogs, only detection, detain, and to, perhaps, kill.

The next day, at 3 a.m., before, it seemed, the rest of the world awoke, we rounded up the dogs and their equipment. This was it. We weren't coming back here, again, and the pride of advancement was challenged with the haunting anxiety of abandoning a comfortable home. It was an all too familiar feeling. Similar to the way I'd felt leaving home for my Air Force induction. I wanted to move on, yet weary the uncertainty of the future.

Aboard the transport truck with me, King, outfitted in his muzzle and short leash, was positioned between my legs. He nudged my foot with his muzzled face, and I instinctively reached down to rub his head. This simple ritual had evolved into a symbol of encouragement between us, and at that moment it was very appropriate. I gazed down at my big buddy. "Everything's gonna be fine," I whispered. He nuzzled my leg as if to respond, *I know.* Comforted, I bent over his head to 'nuzzle' him back.

We reached the encampment, located within the deep forest of Camp Bullis, and unloaded the equipment. Luker and I made sure our modest patches of ground, sheltered by parchment roofs, were located next to one another so our dogs would have company. It was funny, but as Luker and I grew closer, so too did the friendship between our dogs. We together formed a very imposing combination. King and Diablo were, large, powerful, and extremely proud. They were two rulers who openly advertised their nobility.

Each handler scratched out his dog's territory and arranged its equipment according to the training staff's instructions. The encampment was designed to demonstrate that the "easy" part was over. This was the environment K-9 would work in. "Get used to it," yelled the sarge. "When it gets cold, we get cold. When it rains, we get wet."

The usual comforts of civilization were rarely supplied, and when they were, it was our own handiwork. However, for each luxury there was a price to pay, so in most cases we decided to go without. That was the practical thing to do. We worked nights. Days were for preparation and as much rest as possible, but with someone else always up and working there wasn't much sleep to be found. Three to four hours was heaven. Anything after that was asking too much.

"What? You want to sleep all your life?" was the typical retort, and if someone got cranky, the other guys would either ignore him or make it worse for the guy with a stream of relentless ridicule.

Other comforts were eliminated on the basis of survival. All training was now done at night to adapt the handlers to the dark. Our eyes grew more observant and sensitive while one's sense of smell took up the slack that our site gave away. We learned that the glow or scent of a lit cigarette could write your death sentence from miles away in any direction. As a result, many handlers quit or in my case, never started. Our ears were conditioned to pick up minute sound nuances and to differentiate variations and distortions. Compared to daylight, the night was a whole new world. However, if *my* senses were adapting and changing, they were still no match for the dogs' sound, smell, and sight capabilities.

The following day was our first complete one, and we wasted no time.

After a brief obedience brush-up, which one never stopped training for, followed by some recreation time, the sergeant ordered all the dogs to line up in

26

front of a heavily fortified log fence. We were instructed to latch our dogs' leather collars to chain fasteners spaced along the length of the fence. This was the first time we'd used the leather collars. Previous training had always required a choke collar instead. Now, these large, more supportive leather straps would serve as the canines' working gear. From this point on, the dog would transform into a killer/hunter when the leather collar was equipped. The dog quickly interpreted the difference. Roughly 80 percent of the time, the dog would wear its chain collar, but when wearing the leather one, the canine would come to know he was "on the job".

Similarly, as the collars were switched, the handlers were taught to radically change the tone of their voices to prepare the dogs of possible danger.

We were practicing this technique with the chained dogs when "The Agitator" made his first appearance. A member of the training staff was completely padded, just like the Tech from the demo show, and cautiously making his way toward the dogs. His suspicious movements immediately caught the attention of all the canines, and as the drama of the moment intensified, I found myself in a front row seat.

Kneeling down by King's ear I whispered, "Watch him, big boy. Watch him." King never took his eyes from the approaching figure, but I could tell he had no idea what to expect or how to respond.

The Agitator passed in front of the dogs and some began barking out of shear reflex rather than in response to a threat. King stood his ground but did not bark. I was slightly concerned and made a mental note to ask one of the instructors about it later. However, at that point, my mind was on my partner.

"Watch him Kinger," I said, praying for the agitator to pick on King first.

I yearned to see his reaction, if in fact King did act, and how quickly he'd respond. Judging by his breathing, he was going to do something very soon. His ears were up straight with attention and his muscles coiled, ready to spring.

The agitator chose his first encounter, a dog that appeared to be on the borderline of advancement. He was a sweet dog, too sweet for this, and I sometimes felt sorry watching the handler and his animal. The dog was simply too busy wanting to be loved. He was no killer, and I discreetly shook my head as the dog cowered between his handler's legs, cringing in desperation and fear from the agitator, who was screaming and smacking the canine's nose. I watched King stare, attempting to interpret his reaction. His reserved manner was new to me and I smiled. I guess he still had a few tricks of his own up his sleeve.

The agitator moved through the line of barking dogs, heading for his next target. As he moved closer, I began to fidget more than King. "Come and get it, you bastard," I deliberately whispered. "You're mine and you're meat, sweetie." Talking more to myself than King at this point, I couldn't help but hope that King would pay this son of a bitch back for harassing the other dog.

Instead, the agitator jumped at Diablo, standing right next to us. Luker was shouting and 'Blo held his own, jumping up and down. Suddenly, Diablo caught the agitator's left padded arm and sank his teeth into it. The agitator whooped and hollered, but 'Blo hung tight growling continuously and making Luker look good. He'd have no trouble passing.

Just then, I felt King spring into action too. The agitator, straying just a little too far right during his dance with 'Blo, had come too close to King's measured jump. He grabbed the agitator's right leg and sank his teeth deep into the padding. If not for the protection, the man's bones would have splintered. King never barked, but if I had paid closer attention, I would have noticed the rumbling growl that had steadily magnified as the agitator approached. King seemed furious about the previous dog's treatment too. He wanted this guy bad!

King had waited for his shot. Now Diablo occupied the agitator's attention and, as a tandem, both dogs attacked. King's assault caused the agitator to lose his footing and he fell to the ground rolling and kicking in a cloud of dust. "Get him out of there," the agitator shrieked, but his cries rendered no affect on the two enraged canines. They knew they had him and they wanted more.

The other training team ran to the rescue, ordering Luker and I to call off our dogs, but they were grinning too. Knowing we had two great dogs, they were reluctant to disrupt the aggression. I yelled, "out!" at least four times before King begrudgingly released his victim's leg. Glancing sideways, I saw old Luker already rubbing up Diablo in praise. As for myself, I was fit to burst with pride.

That afternoon, the Sergeant who had served as the agitator approached me and began verbally attacking me about having "better control over my dog." He said King "was not listening to commands," I was going to "flunk out," and that the dog was "untrainable." I was completely stunned by his reaction. He claimed that he took his job seriously and personally, accused me of allowing my dog to attack him, and warned that he'd make trouble if I didn't gain better control over my "mutt." I just stood there, speechless as I absorbed the attack.

After he finished his tirade, I left, but I was very upset. No one else appeared to have overheard. The others continued to go about their business, but I knew they had witnessed the Sergeant explode and I didn't know how to respond to. This particular Sgt. was not a trained dog handler. He had been unwillingly assigned to Camp Bullis and was just making a little extra "easy money" as an agitator for the canine training program. Unless a member of the training staff voiced concern, I certainly wasn't going to make any changes to King's training. He was doing more than I'd ever imagined and now I was supposed to "discipline" him because of this guy? Never!

Upon returning to the barracks, Luker told me he heard what happened. "He's wrong! Besides, he is never going where we're going! I would have you and King with me and 'Blo anytime. We're the team! The hell with that wannabe! Let's get a beer, partner."

"That's a good idea. Too bad our other two partners can't have one with us."

The next day I felt much better as King and I went for our daily walk. During the night, Luker and I came up with the perfect response for my ol' Sergeant buddy. It was so great, but the timing had to be perfect. We should practice more "control," I thought, laughing aloud as King and I walked.

The agitation program continued over the next few days. King seemed to love driving into the padded assailant, striving for more cloth with each lesson. During the last session, he'd adapted his attack to ignore the arm the agitator habitually fed him. Timing his leap, he'd dodged the arm to hit the chest area instead. King's novel approach caught even the seasoned veterans off guard. Temporarily amazed and befuddled, they'd raised an eyebrow. "Well done," was the only reaction they could spit out. I, of course, smiled and just trotted back to my place in line with King, knowing he'd accomplished another spectacular feat. King knew it too.

Chapter VI
THE NIGHT

The following and final week of training was night vision. This program would actually present the experiences we'd face on active duty. From this point on, we'd rarely work in daylight, so the following evening at sundown, all the trainees assembled outside the kennels. It was pouring and I thought of many places I'd rather be. Anywhere! For starters! Muddy tracks plastered the slippery ground. One instructor compared the weather to a Vietnam monsoon. Comforting metaphor. However, the weather was a good test for the dogs. Simulating an actual patrol duty, one could more accurately measure the canines' effectiveness in such horrible conditions.

King and I were assigned to K-9 No. 5 and ordered to patrol a sector approximately 250 yards in length between two trees and a large boulder. We jumped off the truck and circled to the front compartment where the training staff was sitting comfortably. First, I straddled King to strap on his leather collar. Next, I pretended to load my weapon, an M-16 with an empty clip of ten rounds. Immediately, I sensed the difference in King's composure. His breathing grew steely and aggressive. When the Sergeant was satisfied, he left, vowing to return on foot in about an hour. "Stay alert!" he called over his shoulder.

"I have no choice," I answered, "King would drag me all over the place to get a *bite* to eat. Right buddy?" I said, patting his head.

About three hours later, I caught my first taste of King's alert signal. We had been walking, struggling to forget how saturated we were, when I decided to sit down for a second's rest. Approaching a rock, I leaned my unarmed rifle against a tree. Suddenly, King froze like a statue, his head raised while his nose worked overtime. Both ears, like radar antennae, twisted from one direction to another until finally stopping in unison in the direction of his nose. His signal was unmistakable, both fascinating and frightening at the same time.

I had wondered if I would be able to recognize King's alert. Some dogs utilize a very brief alert while others demonstrate a mild signal. But Stevie Wonder couldn't miss this one. I pathetically attempted to spot the danger myself, but I saw and heard nothing through the downpour. The split second that passed as I reached for my radio to call in the alert, felt like an eternity.

Immediately, my response came in. I was instructed to move toward the alert but "under no circumstances" should I release my dog.

Judging by the position of King's head, the alert was on the move. As it crossed my post from left to right, I immediately called for backup and relayed my position. "No, still no visual confirmation. The alert is moving in a northerly direction toward K-9 station No. 6."

I was straining to retain King as I focused on our training and the equipment handling instructions. Had I held King's leash in an ordinary manner, I would have already lost my grip or been flung in the mud by King's strength. Instead, we'd been drilled to turn the handle of the leash inside out and slip our hand into the space provided. This way, as the dog tugged, the gripped leash around one's hand actually tightened.

The alert now appeared to be moving away from my sector toward K-9 No. 6. Soon, I picked up the radio call-in for another handler's alert. King gradually loosened his pull, and I heaved a sigh of relief. Our alert was over. "Good job, big buddy." I never spotted a thing, but, thanks to King, I'd known the enemy's presence.

When the training session ended, the truck picked us up again. We were thoroughly exhausted but giddy about the night's events. The horrible weather was forgotten as the group discussed the dogs' alerts. Only two dogs hadn't picked up anything. Their handlers were disappointed until they were informed that no one had penetrated their quadrants for two reasons: one, the weather was a bitch and two, to test for mass alerts, which occurs when a dog alerts only because he feels his handler wants him to. This phenomenon is triggered when a dog senses his handler's excitement at an impending alert. Either the handler misinterprets his dog's actions or the dog responds to his handler's energy level. Regardless, the entire group was well congratulated for a job well done.

The next training phase was night patrol. This time, each dog and handler walked the 1000-yard trail once rather than over and over again like the sentry exercise. Therefore, in this scenario, the dog gets only one chance to alert and can't adjust to his surroundings, thus handicapping his interpretation ability. For this exercise, one was permitted to release his dog, but only if visual contact was established with the alert. If one lets the dog go too early, one could lose contact with the alert and lose sight of the canine, leaving the handler alone. In addition, one must always establish the alert count. Never release the dog for two or more simultaneous alerts or you risk losing your partner to overwhelming odds. Instead, the handler should always keep his dog, even if just for protection. Above all, one never wants to be separated from his dog.

I found it best to allow the alert to come to King and I because the moment we chased our suspicions, we became the prey, and the weaker party in a confrontation. We'd let the alert come to us.

This night bore no resemblance to the previous night's storms. A half moon rose through the stunning, star-lit sky. It was about 10 p.m. but who was watching the time. Tonight it was fun to be out with the dogs. As we huddled together, waiting our turn to walk the line, Luker and I wondered if we'd man the same station if shipped overseas. How cool would that be for the four of us?

Suddenly, I heard my name called. I told Luke to keep my seat warm, reported to the training area, and was tentatively briefed about what to expect. Straddling King, I switched his collar and we headed out.

It's amazing how one's eyes adapt to the night. With clouds reflecting the lights of downtown San Antonio, and millions of stars glimmering in the dark sky, the night quickly assumes the air of daylight. Still, I could only make out the images and discernible shapes of trees and rocks. We'd been walking, very slowly for about five minutes when I detected King's attention on a shape off to the right about 200 yards away. I watched intently, but King's reaction was different than the night before, so I was unsure. As we closed in, I was positive there was a man hiding behind a tree, but King grew less enthusiastic. "Oh shit, " I thought, "he missed one."

However, as I continued to position him in the direction of the tree, I suddenly realized that he was watching another tree about 100 yards further down the path. Stopping to kneel beside King, I mulled over the situation. As long as we didn't move, I thought, no one would spot us. Movement was the easiest element detected at night—not color, not distinguishable marks.

Pertinent questions had to be answered immediately. Was this an alert? Where was it? How many were there? I waited, feeling time was on my side. It had to come out sooner or later. Just one move, and I'd know what we were up against. King, as patient as myself, seemed to prefer the furthest tree, so I opted to watch the nearest one while whispering encouragement in my dog's ear. While he was willing to wait, he had already picked his alert, no question about it. Ten minutes later, King's alert darted around the tree and into a bush about 10 yards away.

At that point, the training Sergeant called me on the radio. He was concerned because the agitator had actually lost track of me and he didn't want the dog to sneak up on him because he was only wearing a chest protector and an arm pad. I called back to assure them all was well. I told them I'd made one visual contact and assumed it wouldn't take much longer. I called in the alert, but added that I might have a multiple alert and didn't feel comfortable yet in my present situation. As a result, I requested backup. The Sergeant praised my reasoning but explained that because this was only a training mission, there was only one infiltrator.

"In that case, I got him behind the bush about 100 yards away."

At that point, the infiltrator jumped, and I released King to capture his reward. After subduing King, I walked slowly over to the location of my alert. I had been wrong and King had had him all along. *My* alert was a tree branch, and it wasn't going anywhere.

As I walked back to the assembly area, two members of the training staff approached me. For the first time they spoke to me about my dog. "He's a special one alright," the staff member said, praising the dog's successful mission.

"I know. I'm just glad I followed him. He's the boss!"

The next night was a replay of all the lessons we'd learned. The exercises were designed to offer the dogs one more shot at the agitator. Funny enough, none of the dogs were afraid of the clown anymore, but it was good exercise for their teeth and legs. In tonight's scenario, we would patrol the location and meet an intruder. Since he would be wearing pads, the dogs were permitted to go off lead and "stop him."

King and I had walked only ten minutes when we confronted the agitator. I stopped and commanded him to "halt," but the perpetrator continued to jumping around, yelling and screaming. In retaliation, I ordered King to attack and he immediately launched a vicious, driving thrust, catching the agitator's sleeve. While the padded volunteer was skilled at giving King a good workout, the growling dog continued to gnaw and gnash. I waited a few seconds and yelled, "stop!" then "out!" King instantly released the agitator. "Heel," I said, and King returned to my side. The agitator, about seven feet in front of us, stood motionless. "Don't move," I told the enemy. Then I dropped King's leash, whispering, "stay, watch him."

King's head never moved as I approached the agitator. Only now did I recognize the man beneath the pads. It was my number one friend, the sarge. The one who told me to "get better control over that stupid mutt or get another dog". I smiled at him, knowing that he was now supposed to knock me down. When it happened, it had to hurt. As I lurched, I swirled around just in time to see an unmistakable tan and black flash pass me by. Before I'd even hit the ground, King had grabbed the agitator by the chest with only the pads to prevent the canine from ripping out his heart.

Now, it was the agitator squealing for help as he felt the dog's teeth penetrate his protective layer of gear. The other instructors told me to call King off and I did, but what a sense of retribution. I had never been so proud of King.

The training process was complete. The real world awaited us now, and deep in my heart, I knew we were ready. Two things were already apparent to me. Number one, I had made the right choice by volunteering for K-9. Secondly, since the day we'd met, a very special bond had now been forged between King and I. One bigger than I had ever expected; one bigger than I had yet to realize.

Now, there was but one thing left to do. As we loaded our equipment on the trucks before heading back to our base kennels at Lackland for further instructions and new orders, both Luker and I made sure we were the last ones to board. The entire training staff was assembled in front of the one-story wooden structure that had housed the dogs during the last two weeks at Camp Bullis, and we relayed our thanks and regards to the camp's personnel. At the same time, I scanned the crowd, looking for one staff member in particular—my ol' sarge buddy. I was afraid I'd missed him when he suddenly emerged from one of the buildings.

As the trucks lurched forward, beginning to depart, both Luker and I called out "Hey, sarge!" As he turned, both King and Diablo rose from their sitting positions. "Our dogs just wanted to tell you what they think of your obedience control." With that, both dogs cocked their hind legs, pretending to "piss on it." As we waved, the rest of the staff laughed hysterically at our little *bon voyage*. Much to his credit so did the sarge. Realizing what we'd trained the dogs to do, he smiled and waved back.

Chapter VII
ORDERS

"As long as there is men who hate and destroy, we must have the courage to resist. The South Viet Nam people have fought for many long years. Thousands of them have died. Thousands more have been crippled and scarred by war. And, we just cannot now dishonor our word or abandon our commitment, or leave those who believed us and who trusted us to the terror and repression and murder that would follow. This then, my fellow Americans is why we're in Viet Nam."

President Lyndon B. Johnson:
The Directorate for Armed Forces Information and Education
July, 1965

Two days later we got our orders. Everyone had an "A.P.O., San Francisco" on them and we immediately knew what that dreaded address meant. South East Asia, Viet Nam. "Well, we might as well get it over with." I said to Luke. "Yeah, we knew it was coming. It might as well be now, while everyone's here!" One of the guys said that he heard we'd be joining up with a larger force of about 300 handlers from bases around the nation to go over. All branches will be part of the task force, Army, Marines, Navy and Air Force.

"That'll make Taylor feel better, that his Navy dudes will be along for the ride." Seaman Taylor was the only Navy that was with us during training and he took an unending verbal good-natured beating from everybody.

"Well, it looks like we've been formally invited to the 'Big Dance'. According to these orders they give us two weeks leave and then, three days to get ready." The Sgt. said, as he came out of his office, where the bulletin board was, on the wall. "You guys go home and be back here on Sunday, 12 September."

I was happy to go home for a while but after saying my "good-byes," I was getting kind of antsy and soon I started missing the big guy and decided to get back to camp, early. He was there in the kennel and as soon as he saw me, King jumped up and welcomed me back wholeheartedly. I guess he missed me too!

The first thing I did was grab a leash and took him out for a walk to get us back together, again. We ran into some of the guys and we said, "hello." It was a few days before we all were to be back but some of them were getting to feel like me and were already drifting in, "Let's just get this thing over with."

I brought King back in after an hour or so; changed his water and brushed him up. He looked simply "regal" in his stance and I had a lot of feeling and pride for him. I went and checked Diablo and he seemed glad to see me, too. I would never attempt to enter into his area but I did manage to change his water and clean out his stall. I was hoping for Luker to get back soon and we could get a beer, together.

The next day, I entered the kennel and took King for a long walk. I again felt bad for Diablo and the other dogs but I knew their handlers would be coming in soon, enough. I just wanted some quality time with King and I think he liked that. I did go over to say hi to "blo" and his wagging tail acknowledged me. I did give him some extra biscuits I had for King and I knew he was ok."

After some exercise and some jumping around King and I just fell into a slow walk around the area. I had visited his home during my leave and I found out all about his background from the farmer who gave him to the K-9 program. As I was talking he listened and I could swear he look up at times with that kind of, "how you know that?" look. I really had to laugh at his facial expressions. His family told me from the beginning he was a "case to handle". He was always investigating things and upsetting the other animals.

"Causing trouble was what he liked to do"! And, being "chased by all the other bigger animals around the farm. I knew King was for me. I had what I was looking for in a highly spirited partner and we were going to share some crazy adventures, together. I wouldn't have had it any other way.

That afternoon Luke came in and now the "four" of us were back together, again. It was good! Others now started to arrive and soon handlers whom I never saw before started reporting for duty. In the group were the first handlers, now, who had given us the demo show and we all greeted each other, now as "brothers" very enthusiastically. Many others from all the branches, not just Air Force, had joined us. It was always clear to us that K-9 was a multi-purpose, multi-organizational "special operational force". This airlift, code name, "Operation: Pipeline" showed just how trans-operational, we were. And, our mission was crucial to the conflict we were all now preparing to join. In the next few days we were to embark on one of the monumental experiences of our lives. I hoped we were ready for it.

Chapter VIII
ON OUR WAY

Wednesday, 15 September 68':

We were all packed and the last thing was to prepare the dogs for the two-day flight, across the Pacific. That morning we all trooped down to the kennels and leashed the dogs, for their final walk. King was "droopy" and I knew the medication that had been mixed in with their morning food was quickly taking affect. We were then told to bring the dogs over to the "docking" area. This was an area behind the kennel with a raised platform. It was this platform that allowed us to board the transportation truck easier. There were all metal cages arranged four across and three up with each dog's name and serial number on them. We first lined up for one more quick shot the veterinarian gave to each dog. It was all we could do to get the dogs into the cages before they all were sound asleep. I patted King's head and rubbed his neck just as he closed his eyes for the trip. I knew he liked that and would be ok. We then hung around watching the derrick pick up each cage and place it on the flat platform. King was placed on top of two other containers and on the left. Diablo was positioned right next to him. With any luck they would sleep the whole trip. But, I would be there and be the first thing he would see, when he woke up. We all then boarded the buses and the twenty-one-vehicle convoy started its trip to Kelly Air Station where three C-130's were all ready and waiting for us to load-up.

In an hour and a half we took off. Some of us would never come this way again. I silently said a prayer upon take-off then got up and went to the back of the plane, around all the covered equipment and the sleeping dogs. I reached under the canvas where King would be and felt his coat up against the gate. He was resting and I murmured, "that's right, big buddy, you sleep now. I'm going to need you, big and strong." I turned and was strangely comforted to see Parker already with the deck of cards in his hands and a small package in front of him greeting and smiling to everyone trying to get a game of cards going. God Bless! Good things NEVER change. Approximately, ten minutes later the sound of shuffling cards and money exchanging hands could be heard. I knew I would probably join in, later, but for now, I sat back down and read a magazine I had bought. Luker was reading some crazy book about ghosts and we both had to laugh. He said it was pretty decent and told me to read it when he was done with it. After a while we both took a nap.

GOONNGGG!!!! The plane's alarm went off to alert everyone we were about to land. This was it! If there were any doubts, now, or imagination theories, they were immediately dismissed.

We had landed twice before. The first time was at Pearl Harbor. The same Pearl Harbor I've seen so many times before in war movies and news documentaries about World War II. This seemed like a movie too! Here I am, a boy of seventeen. First time, actually, away from home and I was undertaking an adventure some people only read about or watch, with their girlfriends in the movies. Then "portraying" the hero after the show, saying what they would have done. HA! No heroes, here!

I myself would have liked to do some "sight-seeing." But, we couldn't leave the flight area. It was dark and all anybody could see was the big city lights of Honolulu. Some one made a crack about "how cheap was this tour," if this was all we were to get, for our money? Here we were, in Hawaii. The land of Elvis Presley and McGarrett, of "5-0" and what were we doing? I walked over to see a better view and I promised, one day I'll be back, here. It really looked like "paradise." Luker said how does one get "stationed" here? Wow! What "duty" that would be!

We boarded back on the plane about two hours later and took off for Wake Island, our next scheduled stop. I remembered that old war movie, starring William Bendix and Brian Dunlevey and I immediately felt like being there, watching the Japanese inching closer and closer to their conquest, just a mere 28 years ago.

I was actually walking on the same ground and probably looking at the same vegetation and trees that saw the whole thing! I remember my mother and my father discussing this movie and, now, I am actually HERE! History always held a strange fascination for me and now I was "living" it.

We got back on the plane and headed for our last scheduled stop, Okinawa. I checked on my "sleeping" partner. He had shifted but was still knocked out and resting comfortably. I wanted to be the first thing he would see when he woke up. Then, I figured, he'd really "tear me a whole new a—hole, for doing this to him. Ha! I sat down and joined that card game, now. Still going strong.

Okinawa was probably a combination of the two previous stops. The hustle and "bustle" of Pearl Harbor was quite in evidence yet so was the "historical" and the "Mystique" of Wake. It was very evident, if for the first time, we "weren't in Kansas, anymore"! Quite a whole new awareness seemed to take over the senses and surroundings. I don't know if it was because of us drawing ever so nearer to our own destiny or what, but it was there and it seemed to hit everybody. No more joking and no more card playing. Everybody got noticeably business-like and silent.

I didn't know it then but we had "lost" our innocence. We boarded that plane one last time and when we will land, we will be in a life or-death struggle … a WAR!

Chapter IX
ARRIVAL

As the big C-130 landed and came to a stop, I looked at Luker and said, "This is it!" He just nodded. The engines started to simmer down and the two huge sliding doors cranked open to expose our first view of our new "home" for the coming year. One plane had already landed and the guys were already milling around as they started unloading the equipment from the storage compartment in the underbelly of the big transport. I came down the movable stairwell and the first thing to "hit" me was the tremendous heat and all the noise emanating from this very busy airbase. As moving and occupied as any I ever saw and that included some busy ones in New York City. Speaking of which, I looked at my watch. I never changed the time I had when we left, so I was actually still on New York time. I went over to one of the soldiers unloading the wooden slips from the plane to ask if I could have the time. He told me it was 11:35A.M. I looked at my watch and I had 11:35, also. I quickly realized that we were 12 hours ahead of New York time. Since this was Saturday morning, at home, it was 11:35P.M. Friday night SCHEEEESCH! And, I knew where everybody at home, was and what they were doing. I was clearly half way around the world! And, what the hell was I doing here?

I walked over to Luker to tell him and he started to talk about how different the terrain was here. It was all **so** "twilight zone" different from a landscape from the States. All hilly and mountainous with green vegetation everywhere. I never saw "green" covered mountains before or valleys so thick with trees.

These trees had branches that seem to bend and move by themselves and they were covered by long green, stringy leaves that formed a "curtain" type of impenetrable shield. Nothing like we ever saw before. We just gave each other a look that pretty much summed it up, "Oh SHIT!"

A group of guys, now, were heading towards us and introduced themselves to everyone. I heard the third plane coming in for a stop with the other component of the task force and the engines created a "havoc" effect with it's noise and the wind. A guy came up to Luker and me and shook our hands to welcome us.

"I'm Pete Christiano, I'm from Bayonne, New Jersey. Ever hear of it?"

Luker said, "Naw, Where is it?" I laughed, and introduced Luke and myself. He said to follow him inside the huge hanger type complex that served as a welcoming area. I grabbed a bottle of soda. The whole area was "steaming," heat. Pete said, "you'll get used to it because it never drops below 70' degrees."

You're lucky! This is the "dry season. Wait till the Monsoons come in with all the rain. You'll gladly take the heat." I said, "I believe you.

I glanced out the window and saw them starting to unload the dog's section. I motioned to Luke and the three of us went back outside to "supervise" the unloading. "My Dog's name is Ranger. Good dog." We just nodded our heads. I said I wanted my dog to see me "first thing," if he woke up. Greig Parker, standing there, too, said, "Geez, You want the dog to have a heart attack?" We laughed but I said you're dog would probably want to play cards, when he woke up. Is that what you were waiting for?"

All the dogs were unloaded on the tarmac and from the noise some of the dogs were now awake from the "feeble" barking attempts we heard. Pete asked what the hell kind of dogs made that kind of noise?

"They sound like Chihuahuas." "Yeah," I said, "And they all come from Bayonne." Pete then said, "They must be great dogs then."

I could tell Pete was going to be one of the "good guys". We all reassembled inside the welcoming area and everybody seemed to be in a "giddy" mood. A few laughs were heard and the atmosphere seemed almost "celebrational." I was, but I wouldn't have understood it even if it were explained to me, at this moment. I just attributed it to the arrival and finally getting off the plane and "being here." However, I was to find out there was a whole lot more to it than that.

Pete came in the first group of handlers that arrived in March. I could see how hard that must've been for no precedence and in effect having to "blaze your own trail," in this thing. With no preset guidelines or experience it was pretty much "on the job training." That was rough considering that "Charlie" has been here a lot longer and has been fighting for the last thirty years. They know the terrain and they use every bit of it for cover and the advantage. In equating the "match-up" we had "technology" and "numbers" on our side. THAT'S ALL! The Cong had everything else.

It was never made so more clear when all of a sudden a barrage of mortar fire started landing on the base. It was "organized chaos" all over the place. Everybody running to their "stations" and all activity came to a "screeching halt." There were only about five or six explosions and a couple of wooden and wire huts, called "hootches" were blown up. But, I wondered if that was our "welcoming," from our friendly neighbors. It also demonstrated that they had the capacity to do that, whenever they wanted to. "Very psychological." It certainly kept everyone alert and on-edge. The best thing to do was not to think about it, if you could. You had to relax but be aware, also.

After our "welcoming," we all gathered to hear the Sgt. rattle off names from a sheet of paper and then direct them to assemble in a group and receive further instructions. Luke and I slapped "five" to hear our names called and we walked down the hall into a room with about ten other handlers. Pete was already there and congratulated us for joining his group. We were to stay pretty much in the Saigon area, for the immediate time. The others were sectioned up and were being disbursed all around the country's strategic bases and fortifications that had requested K-9 teams.

We gathered up our equipment and walked out to the tarmac just in time to see the dogs being loaded onto the trailer and being summoned to get on the accompanying "Deuce1/2", a big, dirty green mechanical behemoth. One, I thought could knock over a mountain, if it wasn't careful.

As we got to the back of the truck a familiar old craggy voice squawked, "Com'mon we ain't got all day!" I looked at Luker and we both said, "Pappy!" Sure enough, ol' Walter Brennen, himself was driving, the big truck.

Pete asked, "You know Pappy?" I said we had seen him at Lackland and thought he was a "case." Pete said, "He's a pisser, alright! The only guy I know who could get this "Deuce" stuck in as many mud holes, as he does. At least once a day we have to get the big derrick for the planes to come out and get us out of crap. It's like he has 'radar' to find these holes!"

He says, he "finds them, so he knows where they are for the future."

"Fuller crap", Pete says."

We just get on the big truck and not even seated when the big truck lurches forward and rumbles over the landing strips, in front of on-coming planes and around secured areas, being patrolled by armed security. They wave us through and smile when they see "pappy," driving. Pete says, everybody knows who we are and shows respect. I nod in acknowledgement to that.

I say, "You guys must have made a nice impression since you got here."

"Yeah," says the Sgt.

Matlock was his name. "But, it was 'Nemo', who wrote the chapter. They credit that dog for saving this whole installation, for his action in 66'." Luker said he saw Nemo at Lackland.

"Yeah, so far, he's the dog for this war. Just like "Chips" from World War II and "Stubby," from World War I.

About ten minutes later, despite Pappy's driving, we get to the kennels. One small messy "hootch," that serves as a headquarters/office and some dirt patches of sand-fills, in the rear where the dogs were kept.

As we pulled up all the dogs were barking and you couldn't even hear yourself think. I thought maybe the VC would put in a complaint about the noise. Some of the other handlers were there to greet us. I asked Pete how many dogs we had and he mentioned that they had just lost two but with our arrival we should now be in the vicinity of about 50.

I said, "Pete, but we're the last of this operation, how many were we supposed to be? Sgt. Matlock said, "80." It didn't have to take a "math wiz" to figure out that these guys have been having a hell of a time, of it. I looked at Luker and we rolled our eyes.

Noise now drifts up from the runway. One of the planes that brought us here has now taxied and slowly takes off down the airstrip with more speed it gently lifts off the ground and into the sky. I think to myself, "Oh, well. All ties are now broken, we're here and we're gonna stay here."

"Going north," says Pete. "Probably, DaNang, Maybe, Pleiku."

As in perfect timing another handler, AIC Richards, emerges from the hootch with a cooler full of beers.

Just then we get a phone call. The Sgt. picks up the phone on its second ring and a look of disgust crosses his face.

"Yes, Sir, right away!"

"Ok you new guys get back on the deuce, Pappy get them back to the tarmac with their stuff."

Matlock then turns to Luke and me and says, "You guys are going on a trip," 2-3 weeks "TDY," temporary duty assignment. You'll get briefed on your way to your new location. Oh, by the way, welcome to K-9."

We all reach for a beer and tip to each other. I savored the cold beer going down my throat, but I knew we were way in deep over our heads. No amount of training could prepare anyone for this; let alone a green 17 year old and his 14 month dog.

Slamming on the brakes of the deuce and just missing the waiting plane, Luker and I jump off and gather with a group of about twelve other handlers. We get back on the plane and looking through the small windows watch as they repack up the supplies and dogs and then without a moments break the spinning propellers of the big C-130 go into high speed. The doors close and at once the plane taxies out to the runway. The engines scream and the plane starts down the runway speeding until that now familiar gentle lift tells everyone we're not on land, anymore. Sgt Jack Williams unbuckles his belt first and then motions everyone to come over to where he's sitting.

"I've been ordered to be the NCOIC (non-commissioned officer in charge) for this detail. Let me tell you what we got."

"We've been invited to this place over here in Thailand." He opens his map to the spot and it shows the Southeast Asian region.

"Vietnam is here," he points out with his right index finger, "This is Cambodia, right next door and this is Thailand formerly called "Siam.""

"Not too many people know or care but we've got some pretty important places over here. For one, we got a beaut of a B-52 base right here at this place, "Utapoa." This place also holds our KC-135's, giant Fuel-tankers and a whole lot of oil and fuel." The sgt's finger points to a tip of land on the Gulf of Siam, about 80 miles south of Bangkok, the capital of Thailand.

It seems intelligence is swearing "Charlie," the Viet Cong, want to hit this place bad and knock off some of these babies, while they lay on the ground. Make sense since they can't hit them when they're flying."

"We're to come in and make see they don't, until the base can get their own security squared away. I'm told we'll be here for 2-3 weeks. Doesn't sound bad to me. We'd better enjoy it." We'll be landing in about twenty minutes get your stuff squared away and meet me at the hanger office.

Minutes later the plane once again starts to descend and with a slight thump touches ground and taxies to the hanger in the center of this other huge sprawling base. The equipment starts to get put off the plane and the first thing me and Luker do is to see how the dogs are. King is awake but still a little groggy in his mannerisms I just whisper to him I'm here with him and it's "all OK."

We transport the traveling cages by truck up to the far end of the base behind the flight line where all the big B-52's are parked. "My god," one of the handlers says to nobody in particular.

"Jesus, they're big."

Painted in a haunting black and green tone that screams dangerous, the shark-like tails stand tall in the night air and make it look like it's powerful cousin the shark, with it's fin up out of the water. The giant swoop of its wings, however, makes it look like a medieval devil ready to grab you and carry you away, forever.

Stopping on the high ground, we're told to disembark and section off a 20x20 foot area and place the cages in the middle. We double up our 50ft. kennel chain and hammer a spike into the ground. After clipping on the chain, we now open up the doors on the cages and slowly one by one walk the dogs around their new homes for awhile. Filling up huge metal pails with cool fresh water, our partners start to gather themselves and start feeling better. The barking growing stronger and announces to the casual observer, "We're here, get use to it!"

The next few days are used to get the logistics covered and to draw up a temporary duty plan to act on and for each of us to know our back-ups and strategy in case of a hit. We hope not to have to use any of it. We're told this is at the very least a 2 week run until their security force can be strengthened. This was a precautionary move only because of all the intelligence traffic coming out saying that "Charlie" was on his way. Brass at Utapoa have made it very clear how they appreciated having K-9 there and that they knew we wouldn't let them down.

I, myself had some reservations, but prayed it would be all right and it turn out to be something I could tell my grandkids about.

The first few nights were quiet enough. It allowed King and I to get together and "talk" this predicament out. I had confidence in him. But, at night when nobody else is around and you're outside the perimeter fence, 1-5 miles into an unknown jungle, pulling sentry duty, you start hearing all kinds of voices and before long all the confidence in the world gets rattled. My main concern was how did King feel about all this and ME??

We kept hearing this talk all throughout about a "BONDING" that takes place between a handler and his dog. I wasn't a genius, but I knew we were in some deep shit and it was going to get in deeper. If we had any chance at all of getting through this, King and I had to become one, or "BOND." These first few nights, also gave me the opportunity to study him and to see all his nuances and movements. I had to know what he was thinking as well as he to know me. We had to know this team could react in a split second and know what we were doing was right. We weren't going to have the time or luxury of worrying about each other when things get tight, only that we knew we could depend on each other, for each other.

King, I learned in training, had a very distinctive alert. Whenever it was something I should know about, say a "human" alert, he would literally look in that direction and shut his mouth. Remaining motionless and sniffing the air, he would just about tell me what it was and where. Only thing more, sometimes would have been, how FAR AWAY.

But, how did he feel and did he feel the same way about me as I did about him. King was a smart dog. I think he knew what it was we were in. My answer to all these questions and doubts came the next night, on patrol.

We were on beach patrol on this beautiful moonlit night. Hard to believe we were in a war-zone. It's been quiet all night. Not even any planes taking off or landing. We would be the first to know since the huge giant runway abruptly ends where the beach begins and then all you had left was the beautiful tranquil waters of the Gulf of Siam.

To keep the night going for me I picked up a small, transistor radio and tucked in my left breast pocket of my jungle camouflaged fatigues. I played it just loud enough for me to hear. I had tunes, now.

It was getting to be about 3A.M. or about and King and I stopped right at the tip of the runway. We sat down on some rocks and I got out some water and gave some to my partner. While he was drinking, I got up and just took in all this humanity and its incalculable vastness. What a sight to behold. A huge picture it told. A city with a million lights and sounds yet completely enveloped in the darkness of night.

I sat down on these rocks and started playing with King's neck and head. He always enjoyed me sprinkling a little water on his head. It seems to cool him off. This time however, he jerks his head up and looks out into the water. I follow his lead but at first I can't see anything. It was, however an alert, as big and definite as I ever saw one from him.

I gulped and as I was just about to call in the alert, when way out in the Gulf, oh 5 miles, maybe more a light appears in the night sky. Just behind this light and to the left, but further out, in distance, another light flickers on.

I pat King on the head and try to calm him down.

"OK, big fella." We got him. Just a plane, coming in to land." I figured however we better move or else these big birds would be flying right over our heads and low enough to shake hands with the pilots. I get up and gather my equipment when I realize King is frozen solid, as if in a trance. He's never seen something like this before and he's in a state between fear and denial. I kneel down next to him and try to comfort him but he can't take his eyes off the lights. And, now they're coming in lower and faster as they approach for landing. Four lights now and the first one is about a mile away and coming closer. I can feel King actually shaking, but he won't move.

There was just no way I was going to allow this to happen, now. I had to be assured King wasn't afraid of anything. He had to be fearless or at least have this confidence in himself and us. I pushed aside all the equipment and if King wasn't going to move, then I wasn't going to force him, or was I going to leave him.

I knelt down beside him and cradled his neck with my left arm. I started calmly speaking to him for encouragement. The first light was now about two hundred yards away and we could hear its engines, screaming in its descent. As the plane got steadily closer, I got closer to King and hugged him tighter. Still whispering soft words of encouragement. The plane crept closer and closer and we didn't move from our original spot, at the foot of the runway. The unmistaken form of the landing B-52, like a swooping steel gargoyle with its extra long wingspan, was now about fifty yards away and the noise and wind was overpowering. Yet, King and I stayed. The big bomber overtook us in one huge rush of wind and noise, no more than maybe twenty-five feet over our heads. An unbelievable sense of declaration was drawn and declared as I screamed, in defiance, yet I couldn't even hear myself. I jumped up with my fists clenched and punching the air. King was now out of his trance and barking and jumping all around as the B-52 landed about thirty feet away. We now turned and crouched down for the second light, approaching fast. I noticed King was now up. And he was breathing heavy, as if he was taking in air into his lungs for fight. He wasn't shaking anymore, just watching the light coming closer and closer. I knelt down beside him, again, my left arm over his shoulders. I was whispering, not encouragement but to get ready for him to battle. As the second plane swooped in to land, I could actually see the pilot looking at us in disbelief. He must have seen a crazed look on my face looking back at him. King was now barking and swirling all around trying to get at the plane, noise and all. I praised him and was satisfied he was going to be OK. But, we weren't through, yet. The third plane was now coming in. And, King wanted him bad. I could tell he wasn't going to be happy until he gave one of these "jokers" a flat tire. Which, I could swear, he was going for. Now, as the third and fourth plane landed King was actually jumping up in the air, after the big planes.

"How dare they try to scare me and what a fool I was in fearing them," was now what he was demonstrating and telling me. The last of the planes had landed and King had his tail raised high, in victory. He was pretty happy with himself. Me, I was pretty happy, too. I was very proud of the big guy. But, I also was shown how he felt and his faith in me, not to betray him, too. I believe at that moment we had bonded.

The pilots, oh, I feel they had something to talk about, too!

We soon after got word that we were going back to Saigon and that our job here in Thailand, over. Everything came down nice and peaceful, after all. I wouldn't have minded if we had stayed a little bit longer, but it was time to move on.

Chapter X
SETTLING IN

After getting back to Ton Son Nhut, the next few days were used to settle in. We cleaned up and laid out our dogs area at the kennel and were transported all over the installation's facilities; the movies, post exchange, NCO club, and airman's club. The post office and mess hall were also on the tour.

When we got to our living quarters, we found our arrival was greatly anticipated by the local merchants. These were the local people who passed "security clearance" and were allowed to conduct business on base. Here, we followed Pete's encouragement and selected his people to act as our "house people". They would come in and keep our "hootch" in clean and in order and do our laundry, for a small nominal fee each month. It was a "cut-throat" business for these people who lived by what wages they could get for this service Other "locals" could be found just about any place around the installation and it really made me feel odd to see so many of them everywhere. I just hoped they all passed security!

Pete and the others had to go to "work" so they left us to get settled in and Luke and I walked over to the chow hall. They were having "liver" and we saw one of our guys, John Hudson walking out disgusted. I asked if it was worth it and he said "Hell no." We then said what the hell and went over to the airman's club for a hamburger and few beers. It was a good choice. We met a couple of more K-9 there and had a good time.

It was about 9 P.M. when we started hearing explosions and small arms fire coming from off base in the jungle. We went outside and I heard someone say, "They're busy again, tonight".

The next morning everybody came back. They looked tired and filthy but Pete reported, "no one got hurt." A five-man "sapper" team tried to infiltrate the fence just outside the hanger area, where they repair the fighters. Pete's dog "Ranger" picked up the alert and along with a back-up team, called "K-SAT," caught up with them before they could do any damage. One of the explosions we heard was the infiltrators blowing themselves up. They would rather do that than be caught prisoner after their detection. Pete thought, however, they were just afraid of "pappy's" driving. That helped to lighten things up a little, as they all started to drift off to sleep and for a well deserved rest. We new guys left them alone and headed out to the kennels to see the dogs.

King was in good spirits after fully waking up from his sleep. I unhooked him from his kennel chain and walked around the area a little bit. From his reaction, I could tell he knew he wasn't in "Kansas" anymore. But, he adjusted quickly and that made me feel a whole lot better.

After I hooked King back up I walked into the kennel hootch and overheard the lieutenant saying that now we had almost a full company. He could see the men getting some time off from duty. They had been on full alert since "TET," which was six months ago and had been working practically every night since.

"They sure could use some "R&R," for sure," Sgt. Matlock said.

"Five days would be like a vacation for these guys", thought the lieutenant.

"OK, post it up on the board, senior-timers priority and then the "May squad," next. Let's also work a weekly night off for them, too!" Pick a schedule for the guys to choose from. Just make sure everything is covered."

I went outside and told Luke about the plan and he said let's get the same day. I said, "Cool, but, let's get Pete, too"!

"He knows the area since he's been here since February". We didn't have a problem with that and we gave each other "five."

A few days passed and we were getting ready to go on our first "watch". We had gone into town outside the base and I was amazed at all the hustle there was. It seemed everybody had an angle and for the right price anything could have been bought. I got a kick out of the reproduced copies of old records on tape that was available. I had to admit this society's determination to make "orange juice" out of "oranges" for survival, really captivated me. They were the ultimate entrepreneurs, even before the word became fashionable. They could replicate anything and for the right price could bargain a very advantageous outcome. I had to admit a growing respect for these people. They were obviously very glad to have us Americans there, but I was becoming convinced whoever was there they would have found the same situation. If the enemy was of the same "ilk," I was beginning to suspect we were in for a lot of trouble. For what I first understood these people to being backward and ignorant, I now found them to being humble and very respectful. They were also very bright, cunning, fiercely competitive and extremely proud. And, they learned very quickly!

Chapter XI
SENTRY

The moment that finally defines K-9 finally comes to King and I. We join the rest of the company and go on our first watch. We all jump on the big "deuce ⸺" and with "pappy" driving we leave our "living area" and head out to the kennels.

On the way we make our routine stops at the mail office. Since we only just got here, I don't expect any mail so I stay with the truck. As we wait for the other guys to get their mail from home my eyes catch the American flag flapping in the gentle breeze of the oncoming night on the tall flagpole in front of the postal hootch. Along side of it is the flag of The Republic of South Viet Nam. I get a little chill at the footsteps in history I'm following in representing my country and I feel pretty good, too, at the thought of our mission in assisting and defending this country.

At the exchange hootch we pick up whatever will get us through the night. A pack of gum or a Hershey bar usually does it for me. But, for others, still, smoking a pack of cigarettes is a "must."

We now drive up the small incline to the "kennel hootch" and we can hear all the dogs barking crazy. It seems they know, too, this is it!

Posted up on the wall, in the "living area," I was posted on K-9 #4. This is an area just over the bluffs, overlooking the flight assembly line. My area of patrol would be approximately 200yds.accompanied by K-9#3 and K-9#5 on either side of me. I feel reasonably comfortable knowing I'm not totally alone. But, then I'll be with King, too!

We all carry a little personal radio for a little divertissement and at 12 A.M., midnight, the start of the new day's broadcasting begins with a drum roll and then a man's voice:

"FROM SAIGON, AMERICAN ARMED FORCES NETWORK", then the playing of the National Anthem.

I must admit that for the first time, I really "listen" to this and I am very "moved" and extremely proud of what has happened for me. I sit down on a rock for a few seconds and rub King's head gently.

"FROM, SAIGON…"

I guess I really am an American, after all. I'm a long way from home and in a very foreign land. But, I've answered my country's call to "serve."

When K-SAT comes out to see how everything is going, I feel even more proud to be a part of this American team. I report my post and then confessed that I was very glad the first night was "under my belt." It was a rather uneventful night, which I was also so very "thankful" for. The sarge acknowledged he always feels that way on a quiet night. I asked how Luker was doing and he said "fine."

"We're very happy and lucky to have you new guys with us". That made me feel good and I gave a good tug on King's coat and a pat for "well done, boy."

The first sliver of dawn starts breaking through the darkness and all is quiet.

The next few nights are equally quiet but we keep getting reports of increased activity in some of the other outer regions and I wonder how some of the other guys are doing. The VC is great at creating chaos and just the right "climate" so a guy could never fully relax. He can jump out and strike at any moment, anywhere. They really are all over and it's in their strategy to wear you down both physically and mentally. Even, psychologically.

I write to a couple of guys that came over with us and who were deployed further on "in-country," but I never get a response. I guess the mail is more difficult to get through, in country, and so I concentrate on writing home and hope to get some friendly responses. It's good for "morale". I never completely understood that until I got here. But that's how important the mail can be. No one likes to feel "forgotten."

We keep getting news reports about how it seems everybody is against this war, back home. I always ask how everybody can know so much, so far away as they are? It seems to me the ones talking the loudest never got to come over here. Who are these people to question our country's decision? When I ask, they always quote somebody else but can never answer for themselves. That to me is phony. I want to feel as if we ARE making a difference, here.

Some teams start going on patrols with different outfits and sections that request K-9 and that kind of breaks up the usual "sentry" duty. Now we'll go into areas that can be reached only by 'copter and settle in for a day or two, depending on the mission.

"Charlie" has had a long time to set up their networks and fortifications. It takes K-9 to find them and flush them out. Otherwise, an average G.I. could walk right past them and would never know it. The VC can also adapt to the surrounding terrain. Their tunnel systems rivals the New York City Transit. And, I guess, their "trains" run better, Ha!

Most of the handlers that go on these missions are the veteran dog teams that have been together a long time or have had experience at such jobs. Luke and I have a ways to go before they get to us, so we just continue sentry duty. Which is ok with me.

After a few weeks Luke, Pete and me go into the little village outside the base to walk around. I am amazed at all the farmers as they bring in their crops to sell. I buy some and watch how the other villagers sucked the juice out. But, when I try it everything falls apart and I look the fool. Everyone laughs and congratulates me for trying. The villagers who always seem to frown when foreigners past by smile and bow their heads in friendly acknowledgment.

Pete laughs and says, "You've made some friends, 'DEE'."

I say it's because "everybody loves a fool." But Luke interprets, "No, it's because they see you JOINING them."

That seems important to them.

"Whatever", I shrug, but feeling pretty good.

During the next week our only encounter was with a small barge with four snipers, who thought they get by us by using the small creek behind the garbage dumps and is adjacent to some fuel tanks. They wanted to get in quick and cause a little rumpus. They hadn't figured that was also K-9 #31 post.

It was about 2 A.M. and all was pretty quiet. I was sitting on this rock patrolling K-9 #8. It was a beautiful star-lit night and I was rubbing King's head and telling him about some people back home. He always seemed to like listening to my stories about home. Either that, or it was me "rubbing his head." Anyway, he was always very "patient" and never showed any irritation King's personality was really very even tempered.

We just finished a little snack and I gave him some water, when over the radio Ike Knowles calls in an alert. I jump up immediately, only because sometimes one alert could be a "decoy," for another, bigger one, somewhere else. Everything seemed OK and King didn't look to be interested in anything in particular from our new perch on top of this big boulder, that commands a magnificent view of the area. I hear K-SAT's response over the radio and hear "pappy" yelling something, in the background, and I smile. K-9 #31 is on the other end of the installation and I know that if anything should happen, now, over here, we're on our own, except for a possible backup from security on the installation. From what I saw of those guys, they'd shoot me, with all their "keystone" antics. "No", I decided if that ever went down, "I'd try to get back myself or try to team-up with another K-9 team or, better yet, just "dig a big hole." A guy must always have a "plan."

Listening to all the commotion on the radio, I have to lower the sound even lower than usual. I make my way closer to K-9 #7 area, hoping he'd be around, somewhere. Soon after, I spot King's alert and although it coming from where K-9 #7 should be I whistle, while I crouch down by a big tree. Big John Hudson comes out with his dog, Buster and says, "Yo!" We stay about five paces apart because King and Buster don't seem to get along to well, together. We start talking and continue to listen to all the stuff happening over on the other side. Hudson asks, "What happens if they ever get in or get the coordinates and blow the mail-room up?" I say," Man, don't even think about it. They WIN!"

John asks if I'm going to the "movies" later on that day. "They have a one o'clock showing of "the Good, The Bad and The Ugly" with Clint Eastwood. I said, that sounds good! Count me in! He says to be ready by 12:30 and a few of the guys are already going. I say, "Great, I'll get Luke and Pete, too."

The show, over on the other side, sounds like it just about over and I tell Hudson, I'll see him, later. I walked back to my area and listened to some music over the "Armed Forces Radio."

Chapter XII
"CLINT"

The next day about ten of us wake up early and head on over to the movie theatre. This is a ply-board built structure that also doubles as the "House of Worship," on Sundays. It's strategically located in the middle of the sprawling base and really fulfills many objectives. But, for now, it's the "cinema."

I've been looking forward to this because of off-'base activities have been hampered by Viet Cong movement and it has been "highly advised" not to go into town, for the moment. One guy suggested that we'd be allowed to bring our dogs into town with us. That suggestion didn't alter the Captain's thinking, however.

We go into the movie and I sit with Luke and Pete. Somebody says, "This better be good or I know someone who snores very loudly."

Well, I don't know. It might have been the worse movie of all time but we all loved it. It temporarily made us forget everything around us and made us relax and enjoy, again. The situations and outrageousness of the characters, the photography or the music score. It was one of those movies that just "filled the bill" when it came to capturing the moment, that a person just happens to be experiencing.

For me, the music was "haunting." I would have loved to get a copy of the sound track to play, over and over, again. As a whistler, I did manage to reduce the tempo and theme in my mind so now I had a "theme song" to keep me company. And, it may sound funny, but it also fortified my self-confidence. At a few notes, I became one or all three main characters from the movie: Clint Eastwood, Or Eli Wallach as "Tuco" or Lee Van Cleef as "Angle-eyes." As we left the theater we were all kids again, reliving parts of the movie.

It was short lived, however, as we meet reality on the way back to our area. Sgt. Matlock tells us of reports of a VC attack on our big airbase at Pleiku, just north of us. We're immediately thrown into the present. A most dangerous, non-fictitious "Present."

It was a little more hectic around the kennels that night than what had been the previous nights. Something was in the air and we all felt it. Conversation was kept to a minimum and tone was low. Even the dogs barking seemed to have an edge to it.

Maybe it was the Pleiku reports or just the food we had for dinner, but something was out there.

I went to my buddy's area and all edginess fell away as I was greeted with my usual enthusiasm from him. I felt better just being with King. We loaded up the deuce and headed on out into the night jungle and patrol. I had K-9 #7,

54

tonight. Pete was on six but Luke was doing # 31, the oil field. We wished each other a good tour and took our rounds on patrol.

It was about 11:30P.M and I was about 3 miles outside the perimeter fence when I got king's first alert. It was coming in from the grassy fields, which separates the base from the town. I radioed in my non-visual alert to k-sat, my back-up team. Sgt Matlock's voice immediately acknowledged the alert and called in Pete from K-9 six to act in tandem to my position. I heard Pete's response, but it was going to take k-sat a few minutes to get to us because Pappy had the deuce up to it's axle in mud. Normally I would laugh at the site of something that improbable but, not this time.

I had put king in a lay-down position. I don't know why, but I just wanted not to divulge his presence to anybody who might be lurking out there in the night. I knelt down beside him but he didn't move one speck. I couldn't see a thing but he was unmistakably alerting me to something out there.

Then majestically a group of figures came into sight. I counted five but maybe there were more. All were very quiet and they seemed trying not wanting to be seen by anyone. They were about twenty-five yards away when I called in my "visual" alert, in hushed voice. I then place my radio into its holder. I swung around my M-16 and felt to make sure my 10 round clip was inserted in the rifle. I waited for as long as I could for k-Sat but if I waited any longer the shadows would be right on top of me. So far, they hadn't seen me. I wanted to keep it that way. I was approximately 50 feet from the trail k-Sat would be arriving at. And, I didn't want the shadows to get any closer to me. I knew Pete got my identification and that he, too, was lurking out there. I had to make a decision.

The five shadows were about twenty feet yards away from me when I yelled, "HALT!!" I tried to remember what the hell the Vietnamese translation was, but I couldn't remember anything that mundane in my present state of mind.

At the sound of my voice, however, I got my desired response. They all stopped in their tracks and straightened up. Moments passed by like hours, then all the shadows started laughing and slowly started to move on closer to me and King. He was still in a down position but I could feel him leaning up against my leg and I could feel him growling very deliberately. He was actually telling me he didn't like these jokers. And, neither did I.

The closer they got to me the more they tried to act drunkenly and laughing all the more harder.

I yelled for them to stop, but they ignored my demand and kept coming closer to me. A little further and they would now see me.

Just at this time K-sat pulls up to a slamming stop, behind me. I can hear Pappy cursing and the other handlers on the six-man reaction team jumping off the truck. Sgt. Matlock is now on the radio trying to get me." K-9 #7 where are you. Please come in." I can't respond because if I do that I would now have to put my rifle down and grab the radio out of the holder. A couple of more guys try radioing me but I can't respond to them, either and keep the five shadows in my sights. Even Pete, is yelling: "Come in boy, where are you, son?" My mind goes back to the movie we just saw. Here's ol' Clint wearing his poncho, looking down five guys and, you know, something is going to happen real soon. I can even hear the music. It sort of makes everything surreal.

"I wish I had a cigar, dammit!" I murmur, to myself.

A high pitch whistling noise, now cuts, the night air and into the sky. I know immediately that somebody from behind me set off a "slap-flair." It will reach a certain height into the sky, around 200 feet, and then set off a huge light strapped on a parachute that will turn night into day for about 10 seconds. It'll be enough to decide the fate of this story's outcome.

Pop! The flair ignites and now everybody can see everybody else on this chess field in the jungle.

As soon as the five men see King and I they immediately jump to the ground. Going from left to right in order, the first infiltrator falls on the ground and starts crawling away to the left. I shoot the second man as he swings around and tries to fire his rifle he had strapped on his back. He goes down but I'm not sure how hurt he is. The middle or third man had been carrying a sack on his back. He unloads and drops it and starts to fire his revolver. The fourth man dives to the ground and starts firing his rifle he had behind his back. The last man, on the right, dives for cover and tries to crawl away to his right side. He then gets up and attempts to run away when a huge blast from a M-15 shotgun fires and knock the escaping man off his feet and onto the ground, his neck and head jerking backward from the blast. K-9 # 8 now comes out of the trees and heads off to cover any attempts to flee the area.

King is still in a down position and I'm shooting my M-16 on semi-auto, kneeling next to him, one shot at a time, "pow pow pow pow", to regulate my ammunition.

A rustling of bushes and branches, behind me, and I hear Sgt Matlock's reassuring voice.

"Good work Dee! Looks like you caught a sapper team coming in."

"Five-man demo team, to blow up anything they can," yells Russo, one of the guys who came over with Pete's guys.

"We got them good."

The dark night has reclaimed the jungle terrain as the flair sizzles to extinguish itself out. Matlock signals and everyone gets up from where they had been kneeling. The seven men reload their weapons and then commence firing with everything they have into the area as I point out where I last saw the five infiltrators. Three of us have M-16's, two others have M-15's, which are sawed off shotguns and very effective for K-9 duty. They're great at close range and the other two using their pistols and throwing grenades.

56

The terrific barrage lasts about ten seconds but it was something nobody could have survived. As we're firing, we're moving slowly in the direction of the enemy. We now stop and with flashlights start looking for bodies.

"I got three, … Four," … "five is over there by the bending tree, calls Pete as he approaches the site with his dog, Ranger by his side. Ol' Range, didn't like him one bit, either!"

"Great work," says Matlock, "we got all of 'em"

Security teams now come out from the base and the Captain in charge congratulates all of us. "Good job, you guys!"

I bend over to pat my buddy, King, on the head. "Yup! We done good!"

Chapter XIII
"BOB"

The next few weeks have been heavy and everybody was put on "Maximum" alert, which meant no more days off and a full compliment of dogs on patrol. What made it worse was that Bob Hope was coming in for his annual Christmas show and wouldn't that be the "pits" if we couldn't get to see the show. And "Charlie" did.

It's funny but if I were home I wouldn't have cared two bits about watching Ol' Bob on TV. Probably, unless I was sick or something would I even be home. But now, it had to be one of the most important things in the year to have. THE MAN had a tremendous and grateful audience and I didn't see too many other big stars coming to see us. He was "OK" with us. And, we weren't going to let him down or "Charlie" hinder our show.

The next week we were still getting all kinds of "intelligence" about "VC" movements in the area and we even recalled some dog teams from up-country to fortify our ring of security around the base. Charlie wasn't gonna get Bob on our watch. If they wanted to see Bob, let them get their own TV's.

The night before the daylight taping of the show, two helicopters were to fly in and land in an obscure area off the camp. King and I saw the 1st.copter approach and we wondered back towards the perimeter fence to catch a quick peek. About ten minutes later we get to the fence area and come up on the perimeter security guys. I have to shine my flashlight three short bursts to signal my approaching and I get a shaky greeting from one of the dug-in security. The copter's engines were just winding down as we huddled a few seconds and I asked them if that was Bob Hope. They, on the other hand couldn't get over actually seeing King and I. They had heard we were out "there" but they never saw any of us before and asked "how could we be out in the jungle all night?" I smiled and patted King on the head and told them, "I didn't like people much" and it was better, all around, for it to be this way. I heard one guy tell the other, "this guy's nuts!"

Just then one of the doors open on the temporary shelter and out walks Ann-Margaret. I say, "Holy Shit!" I don't think she heard me as I hear another voice from inside tell her to come back in. That it's not "safe" out there. I laughed for I knew she had three "willing sacrifices," and one great dog, that would have done anything for her safety about twenty feet away and she would never know it. I say "bye" to the guards and tell them to keep their "eyes open" in my best Clint Eastwood impersonation and I head on back out to the jungle to meet up with Greig Parker, K-9 #16. It was now about 11P.M.

A few hours later, I had just given King some water. It's a beautiful night with a nice breeze coming in from the shore. We get to about the middle of the patrol area when King gives me an alert. I said to myself, "Oh Shit!" I pray I am wrong but it's unmistakable. I crouch down immediately in the silent undisturbed moonlight. The only sound was the constant humming sound coming from the base flight line. King had obviously picked up something else. I call in my alert.

"K-9 #15 to K-Sat; #15 to K-Sat. Got a non-visual alert".

I give them my approximately position as being thirty feet off the perimeter road and about half way on my patrol. "Alert is moving and going in an easterly direction, close to K-9 #16." Immediately, Thank God, I hear, "K-Sat.

"I copy and were on our way. Be there in five."

"K-9 #16 did you copy?"

"K-9#16, I copy, but I don't have anything, here.

"K-SAT, K-SAT! This is K-9 #12, I have alert, about 50 yards off perimeter road, visually verified. I count five; count five, and they are coming in. Request back-up."

"K-9 12, this is K-Sat, I'm on K-9# 7 Be at your location in two minutes. K-9 #15 what's your situation?"

I get back on the radio and confirm "non-visual alert" and "No changes, but request back-up from K-9 #16 as a precautionary measure. I hear K-9 16 acknowledge and is "on his way."

I tell Parker to be careful as I settle down next to a big tree and wait, for whatever. I hear the commotion over on K-9# 12 and hear "pappy" yelling and hollering and I laugh a little, but now it's my turn.

I've been watching King the whole time and he never takes his eyes off the small shady clump of bushes about fifty yards away.

To answer my worse fear, I see two men jump out and run for the other bushes closer to the road. Now, I have visual contact and I radio it in.

"K-9# 16, I have confirm visual alert; stay where you are!" 16 would have walked right into them if he continued to use the road. With the fighting and shooting going on over on K-9 12, there would be no way they were going to break away from there and back us up.

"K-9# 16 what's your location as to the road?" "I'm ON the road." I tell him of the two guys in bushes about twenty feet off the road but I suspect more in another further on out about forty feet. Just then the two in the lead group jump up and run across the road toward the perimeter fence. They've gotten PAST us and now there is nothing in between them and Bob Hope and Ann-Margaret, except for two very scarred security guards. It's up to Parker and me to get them.

I look at King and pat him on the head. It's no "game," now and it's certainly NO MOVIE! I jump up and using a clump of trees as cover, I cross back over the road and tell Parker what I need from him which is to cover my back in case my suspicions are correct and there are more guys out there under that second bush. I tell him to move up into a better position by the crossing, in case they come after me.

"I'm going after the first two."

In spite of it being a relatively cool night for the region, I'm in a sweat. I got King on full leash and it's all I can do for me is to let him go. They're still busy over on K-9#12 but for King and me the world is an empty place.

I see both infiltrators crouching and now slowly moving towards the perimeter fence. Amazingly, they still haven't seen me. I'm moving adjacent to their movement and waiting for an opportunity to make my presence known. Just when that will come, I haven't the foggiest idea. It certainly wouldn't be the way Clint or John Wayne would handle this. What would Errol Flynn do in a moment like this?

I didn't want King to see any confusion or hesitation on my part so I kept rubbing his head and patting him down, for both our encouragement.

At about fifty feet from the perimeter fence all the bush and possible hiding places disappears for the vision of the security team stationed there. I knew we were going to hit that clearing pretty soon. But I still kept in the cover of the trees. At that moment, I heard one of the security guards yell out, "Is that you K-9?"

OH, shit! Not only did they give away their positions to the two infiltrators but also, they probably gave them even more information as to the location of their target. I wish I could've smacked them. As it were, my "time" had come, now.

The two sappers had just crawled to the fence when the shooting starts. I hold on to King, now, because I didn't want to get him shot and I just wait. I radio K-9 16 and ask for an up-date and to let him know I was still Ok. He said that my hunch was right and that "three more guys were coming in" and that he was on them. I said, "Let them come in." They'll hear the shooting and try to finish the job in the confusion. "That's when we will hit them."

A PLAN! Finally a plan! Sure enough with all the diversion going on here and on K-9 12, it seems it was these three guys, all along; this mission was set up for. It was these three guys that were going to take out Bob Hope and Ann-Margaret and Miss America I finally sort of "relaxed," understanding the situation, and said, "Shame on them, But, not this time!"

While the security guys and their wild shooting into the dark inadvertently held off the two at the fence, King picked up the other three now ready to join the activities. I knew 16 was probably not far behind them so I circled up and around so as to keep the bright lights of the installation at my back at all times and in the infiltrators eyes. I swing around to be in between the two at the fence using them as "cover" and their three partners. I grab the radio and yell to the security guys to, "Stop shooting. K-9 is in position, Stop firing!"

I could hear the screaming and yelling where the living quarters were. They were all going crazy trying to get Bob Hope outta there.

I wait for the firing to stop and count the three most important moments of my life. No director to shout "cut" if I get it wrong or any "special effects" for this "scene." Rising up out of the grass, I start firing my M-16. In one motion, I release King and radio for Parker to release his dog. I immediately turn around and pump two bursts at the two infiltrators by the fence. They were already pretty much slumped over but this persuaded them to go down, "for good."

Meanwhile, both dogs slammed into the three that were left. I run up to the scene just as Parker gets there and we order the dogs, "OUT!" King comes immediately over to me but 16's dog, Ed, probably had a little more "frustration" built up and it took another "OUT!" by Parker to release his victim.

It took a matter of seconds but we did it! All three men were rather "chewed up pretty much, and I really didn't care to look at them to see King's work, but I got down and praised my "best friend" for a good job and for being with me. Wiping the blood and flesh from his mouth, and with his tail wagging, I silently cried and said a prayer. King would never be the same, again.

Security backup finally gets there and congratulates us on a good job. Even the two guards on the perimeter, who can't seem to either shut their eyes or open their mouth, get in on it. I tell the Captain in Security, "I congratulate the two security guys for detaining them and in assisting us in stopping these guys." And, they get a good welcoming by their guys from behind the fence. But, the Captain looks at Parker and I with our mud and bloody uniforms. He shakes his head and pats us on the back. He knows the truth.

Twelve hours later, we're all in the audience, watching the show, up front and pretty much exhausted. The two guards, all nice and clean get introduced and get to shake hands with Bob Hope and get kissed by Ann-Margaret and Miss America. Pictures are taken and they're the "heroes."

I do catch the eye of one of the guards and he looks at me kind of sheepishly. I just lay prone just off the center of the stage and I smile as I wave at him and give him the "thumbs up" signal. He acknowledges, in turn, with a shake of his head.

The cameras pan out to the audience only searching out the smiling, cute and washable faces, to send home. They don't take our pictures. We know they're overshooting us and we laugh and applaud Bob's, cue-card reading jokes and deeply appreciate seeing the "visions" of Ann-Margaret, Miss America and the Gold Diggers. But our tired, dog scented uniforms caked with last night's mud and blood, are thing's they rather not show.

Oh, a couple of other things the cameras didn't show that day. My partner Greig Parker, K-9 #16, while waiting for the show to start, found this big chair next to the stage and sat down in it, soon finding himself asleep. A lieutenant on the General Staff comes running over and starts yelling at Parker to wake-up and get-up out of the chair. Ol' Gen. Creighton Abrams, himself, eyeing the situation and seeing the K-9 insignia on Parker's muddy and ruffled uniform, pats his junior executive and tells him to leave that man alone, "He's earned the right to sleep in that chair, if he so chooses. I won't bother him." Parker slept through the entire show, Ann-Margaret, and all.

And, the cameras missed something else, King and the other real "heroes" that day as they rested in their kennels for another patrol in just a few more hours.

Chapter XIV
"HANOI HANNA"

"The Conference takes note:

> *The Declaration of the Government of the French Republic to the effect that it is ready to withdraw its troops from the territory of Cambodia, Laos and Viet Nam, at the request of the governments concerned.*
>
> *The French Government will proceed from the principle of respect for the independence and sovereignty, unity and territorial integrity of Cambodia, Laos and Viet Nam.*
>
> *Each member of the Geneva Conference undertakes to respect the sovereignty, independence, the unity and the territorial integrity of the above-mentioned States, and to refrain from any interference in their internal affairs.*
>
> *Prohibiting the introduction into Viet Nam of foreign troops and military personnel as well as all kinds of arms and munitions.*
>
> *That the military line is provisional and creates the necessary basis for the achievement in the near future of a political settlement in Viet Nam, in which general elections shall be held in July, 1956.*

Taken from:

"The Final Declarations of the Geneva Conference"
July 21, 1954.

A few weeks later and everything is ancient history. We now have another "mystery" to sort out.

It's been a while but it's no secret that "Charlie" plays mind games. That's one of their weapons they use against us, twenty-four hours a day. They broadcast a radio station from up north and use this very feminine seductive voice to "talk" to us in English.

I've heard that the Japanese did this in World War II, and they called her "Tokyo Rose." The Germans scored relative success with a guy named "Lord HAW-HAW" against the English, in the same war. We now name our girl, "Hanoi Hanna."

I wouldn't care much about what she says but she plays better music than we did! I enjoyed her music and get a laugh at some of her stories about our "cheating wives and girl-friends" and how all the people back home are demonstrating against our government's illegal war."

I really never knew or understood the beginnings of our involvement in this war. Only what had been told to us by Washington about how we should honor our commitments and to stop Communist aggression. Also, it was reported how one of our destroyers was "attacked" in the Gulf of Tonkin, in 1964, by the North Vietnamese Navy.

I only listened to the music but one night, all was pretty quiet and "Hanna" got on a topic I wanted to hear a little more about, our involvement.

She mentioned how it was "promised" by the Allies, during the World War II that this whole area would finally be a FREE nation and not just a colony of France, if they would help in the struggle against Japan. Southeast Asia had been subjected to almost occupational conditions by the European powers, particularly France. America and England promise these people their own country, again, free of outside influence, with their help in combating Japan. Their great nationalist and leader Ho Chi Mihn committed his organizational skills and influence to put together a national army, the Viet Mihn.

At the end of the war, however and victory accomplished, the new arising enemy became the Soviet Union and Joseph Stalin replaced Adolf Hitler as the nation's number one "bad guy". When Ho approached President Harry Truman the President knew he had to appease the French for their support as a "World Power" and their vote in the United Nations Security Council. One of their "price tags" was that they would retain domination of their pre-war possessions in French Indo-China. (Viet Nam, Laos, Cambodia). Ho tried to speak to the President and even offered Vietnam as a "protectorate" to him, just as the Philippines were to the U.S. The President had made his decision however and in direct helplessness causing a state of shock and anger, by the Viet Nihn. France was given unconditional access to the area and they again assumed control with no indication or concern of the "firestorm" anyone started.

Ho, with no other recourse, now went to the much-despised enemy and asked Mao, of Communist China, for support. To offset this he also enlisted the other Communist giant, The Soviet Union, as a wedge" so as to not be totally dependent or subjugated to Asia's "Colossus of the North." This maneuver and truly ingenious strategy was done with the complete knowledge that Ho was not a Communist; never trusted the Communists and having generational disputes with their northern neighbor for hundreds of years. But, he had no other option after the allies "betrayal."

Although the Viet Cong, as they were now known, wearily accepted the Communist's assistance in food, equipment and weapons, they drew the line when it came to "men." They didn't and wouldn't even trust their beneficiaries, for an opportunity of an incursion into their country. They became so adept at war that in approximately five short years, under the military genius of Gen. Giap and now the "legendary" Ho, they defeated the French and in 1954, literally "threw" the French out, FOREVER. Or so it seemed.

Unexpectedly, however, during the Geneva "peace talks" and the extraction of the French, now, led by the United States, under President Eisenhower, at this time advised by Sec. of State John Forester Dulles and his "Domino Theory," This said in essence that if one small nation in this Southeast Asian area would fall under Communism, all the nations will fall, "as in a line of Dominos". It was now determined, at this treaty conference, to "split the country (Vietnam) in half, at the 17' parallel, the North, under Ho's direction and the South would create the new Republic of South Viet Nam, directed by a propped-up government under a "President" Diem, now, under the direct auspices of the United States.

This had to be a bitter situation for Ho to accept and to see his country split in half after all the promises.

To further cause more insult, the United States forested an agreement of "aid and protection" between "member" nations of this region. The now newly formed South East Asia Treaty Organization (SEATO), which included this new "Republic" of South Vietnam. Malaysia, Thailand, Burma, England, Australia and New Zealand was based on the same premise as The North Atlantic Treaty Organization (NATO), which was to counter the "Cold War" diplomatic efforts of the Soviet Union in Europe and to in effect counteract the "Domino" theory.

Now the U.S. postpones the negotiated national elections, to reunite the Vietnamese nation, in 1956, upon seeing he couldn't win in an election of popular support from the people against Ho Chi Mihn, Diem accused the North of political interference. Struggling to maintain power and receiving indications of the new U.S. President John F. Kennedy's lack of support the commonly known corrupt, yet, anti-Communist, President Diem, was "assassinated" in 1963 and here was the origins of my country's "commitment" to this area of the world.

To the North's credit, although however previously reported they never have capitulated to or become subservient to the huge Communist neighbor, to the north, China.

I really found all this fascinating and very disturbing. I wanted to know more and to follow up on this information but nothing was ever mentioned in the library and nobody seemed to know much about any of this around the base. In the meantime, however, another situation arose much more closer to "home" that directly began to disturb us.

It seemed harmless information and idle "chit-chat" was getting back to "Hanna" and she was actually broadcasting all our innermost thoughts and actions.

I mean harmless stuff was now finding it's way back to "Charlie." And, they were telling us about it! Broadcasting what we had for dinner, or inviting a debate about two basketball teams, the VERY two teams we just argued about that very afternoon, back at the barracks! Wishing us a good and "safe" patrol and then naming our names and posts numbers. Saying how "wrong" we were or gave a "lousy" review to a movie, we just happen to see. This was beginning to shake us up! We had heard about a "bounty" the Viet Cong placed on our heads and we knew we were getting to them pretty good. We had stooped them cold in their strategies and had pretty much taken the night and jungles away from them. But now this was their way in getting to us.

How were they getting all this information about us? It was as if "Charlie" had personally declared war against K9. It WAS getting to be pretty personal between us.

Of course we still had the greatest respect for them but they had to get through us, first, if they wanted to cause their old fashioned damage and terror campaigns, again, as before we got here. We were the first line of defense and alert for our installations and "always up-front" when it came to everything else, from patrols to secret missions. In finding their booby-traps and supply caches in the jungle. K-9 seemed to have shut them down. The V.C. had to get rid of us. But as they say, "they couldn't run… and, they couldn't hide."

It was in "congratulating" SSgt. Cavanaugh, from Atlanta, Georgia, on his first child's birth, that very morning, that got everyone a bit crazy. "Cav" went to the Captain to see if he could get a call through to his wife as he had not received any official notice and to make sure everything was all right. The Captain told him a "military hook-up," to the States called MARS had come in that morning but that he would authorize another and Cav then talked with his wife at the hospital for about twenty minutes. He was "good" after that, but that didn't stop or disclose how the "VC" was doing what they were doing.

We searched everywhere for hidden microphones or anything as to how they could be getting this information. Since we were still on "Alert" and no days off, we had to figure the source had to be "close to us." As mentioned, "Charlie" hated K-9 for the job we were doing to them. Their fear and superstition was so great for the dogs, that whenever we needed to get information from a captured enemy and they wouldn't want to tell us, all we had to do was to march in one of our dogs and the poor guy would start talking about their ancestors. But, now, WE started to feel the "spook" in this game of iron wills.

It got to the point that we began to suspect anyone we talked to. I kidded Luker about "Hanna" having a "Bayonne accent" and I thought Pete was going to hit me! He later apologized and we had a good laugh about it but it just showed how nerves were just a bit frayed, by it all. The only person I did "trust" was King. But, even he was out of "ideas" on this one.

We decided not to listen to "Hanna," anymore. No matter, if her music was better than ours. But, that still never really answered how they "got into our heads" the way they did.

That came three days later when just by accident the Sgt. posted the wrong daily postings on the board and that night it was heard over the radio. Now, it was known that the "spy" was somebody in the "living area." All day long it was "casually" observed to see who was copying the memos posted on the board. Even during chow someone was left behind in position, "shining shoes," to see who looked at the duty roster. Two suspects emerged and were kept under full observation for further information, on how they sent the information along to their "friends" and where. For the next two days, it was casually observed how they mingled throughout the area, undisturbed and never questioned when seemingly to ask harmless questions about home. The men generously told them anything they asked or even shared their mail or photographs with them. And when they thought it was clear, they were observed looking at the duty board for more "information." It was the two "house-girls" who were gathering all the information. The next day while we were sleeping a jeep load of security men pulled up and took them away. We never saw the two girls, again. After a while, we found out they had confessed and they were sent to prison.

Chapter XV
CHRISTMAS 68'

It was now the week of Christmas and New Years 1968. Pete had just left to join a group of paratroopers of the 101st Airborne to help in a "clean-up" near Chu Lai about 50 miles from here and he said it would take a couple of days. Pete and Ranger were a good team and although he never showed much outward affection for his partner, you could tell through that tough New Jersey exterior he loved that dog as much as any of us loved ours.

All he's been talking about, though, is going home in a "short time." The whole first crew that came over in March, now were getting short" and they were letting everybody know it. Now, however, the word "officially" came down that we had to leave our dogs, when we "rotated back to the world." We all heard the rumors and balked at the idea. After all we've been through, how do you leave behind your best friend? We wouldn't believe it until the Captain verified it. It seemed some dogs, up north, had contracted a viral-intestinal disease and it would be almost impossible to detect until the symptoms showed. It would then be too late. It was suggested it would be much too dangerous to have any of the dogs brought back home, to possibly spread it.

That was one story. Another was there weren't any other dogs to be brought over to replace these dogs and it was hoped these dogs would allow another to become their handler. This story was the one that held much more "credence" and belief than the first one. King was 100% and he didn't act or looked sick.

But, it was news like that, that totally put a "damper" on any Christmas festivities for me or for any other handler. That I couldn't take King home, again, just devastated me. I remember that Christmas of 68' being very melancholy. The war seemed to been put on "pause" and the time went dragging by. We all felt deeply that we could work out some sort of arrangement to get our dogs back home.

I spent Christmas night on K-9 #34, which under different circumstances would probably have been one of the most beautiful places I've ever seen. Just like in one of those movies about the islands of the South Seas. I was patrolling on top of a ledge area that had a commanding view of the seashore off to my left and the harbor port to my right.

As the waves broke and came in to the beach in a rustle of foam and power a sort of soothing effect overtook my frustration. My thoughts were about home. A whole flood of memories rose up in front of me and I clearly saw many people who I came in contact with, in some part of my life. Even some of my "escapades." Great harmless kid stuff that I now were glad to have to think back on. But a small nudging wet nose rudely brought me back to where I was. And, right now I just hugged my "big buddy" as tears filled my eyes for my eventual "betrayal."

I kind of played it off, somewhat, when I reasoned that by the time September comes around ANYTHING could happen. I really needed to shake off this depression. A lot more things are going to happen before this was finished.

That cheered me up and I pushed it out of my mind as I opened up "Christmas Dinner." a cold can of "c-rats". Actually, beans and franks in a sauce. I felt kind of "spunky" and decided King and I were going to eat "elegant" tonight. I spread out a little place serving on this rock and with a little music from "Armed Forces Radio" I lit a low and well-concealed fire to heat dinner up special this night. I poured some water for King and when I thought the food was ready I served some to my best friend and I scraped up the rest out of the hot can, while I held the lid. DINNER WAS SUPERB! The atmosphere and service rated a TEN. I must remember to recommend this place to all my friends. The company was "divine" but his table manners needed a little looking into.

Chapter XVI
"SUPER BOWL JETS"

It was now three weeks later and everybody was expecting a rout in the football championship Super Bowl III.

The new upstart American football League Champions, New York Jets, with the new "Johnny Unitas", quarterback phenom, Joe Namath, were playing the Baltimore Colts, Champions of the more established National Football League and quarterbacked by living legend and the "old" Johnny Unitas. My hometown Jets were eighteen 1/2 point under dogs. But, it was clearly going to be a "classic". I was the only "jerk", however, betting for the Jets and I had to support my "homies"! Besides, my man Joe Namath even "guaranteed it!

That was all I said as the bets kept coming in for Baltimore. It was about $400 and I knew I couldn't handle any more. If the Jets lost, I'd be broke for the rest of the year! I tried to persuade Luker to back me up but he came from Philly and he "wouldn't even think about it." All week I was approached to make a bet, like I was the only one in the world even thinking the Jets had a chance in this game. "Man, Baltimore is going to score, DURING THE NATIONAL ANTHEM." I kept hearing it all week.

The big game finally came. I was on K-9# 31, that patrol and right next to the fuel depot. The stench from the garbage dump, nearby, stunk to "high heaven" and I figured it was sarge's way of telling me how stupid I was to bet on the Jets. Even King wouldn't "talk" to me. But that was ok.

The Jets scored the first touchdown of the game with a run to the left by fullback Matt Snell. And, "Wahooooo!!!!" could've been heard for miles, as I shouted with glee!

King probably thought I "really bought the farm" the next time the Jets scored, as he jumped up on my chest and the two of us danced, "to the music." "Charlie" must've had the Jets, too, because all night long, not a peep out of him. They had to be watching on TV, slugging down some "brews" over some "cow-pod," themselves, somewhere.

The best part, I thought, was that this is being broadcast, "live" with the twelve hour difference in time. It was 4 o'clock, Monday morning, here. But it was 4 o'clock, Sunday afternoon, stateside. That means a lot of these guys who wanted to bet the Colts and work days are sleeping now. They won't know the out-come of the game and when they hear it this afternoon, on the "replay," they'll figure it to be "live." I could make a bundle on this. Again King and I "Boogalooed up Broadway." We were in the "chips," baby! That first touchdown gave me a 25 point lead with the "spread" and forbidding a total collapse we just had to play them tough defense, the rest of the game.

When the Jets scored again to make it 13-3, in the third period, I was "counting my money."

Daylight was breaking and pappy was now picking up all the teams on the duece1/2. As I got on the truck, nobody would even look at me. Not even Luker!

I said, "Ok, you guys. The brews are on me". That's when everybody started laughing and congratulating me. It was a good jovial and wisecracking ride back to the kennels, until we got there.

Sgt. Matlock met the truck as we backed in to the docking area.

"Put your dogs away and come into the hootch as soon as you're squared away."

He was very serious and there was no more signs of a happy Super Bowl win. I looked at Luker and he just shook his eyes. As we did our routine for the dogs of giving them water and patting them down for their day's rest, Ike calls everybody to get in the hootch.

"OK, I'll give it to you straight. Pete got busted up while he was in-country." Luke and I were sickened.

"They're bringing him in for a short layover at the hospital until they can "air-vac him to Japan."

"His guys suffered 70% casualties. It was a mess.

"Dee, I know you and Luker were close to Pete. I'd like you two to get his things together and see him at the hospital when he comes in. The rest of you guys leave them alone. The hospital isn't big enough for all you guys to go over there. Let them do their job. You guys can relay any messages for the rest of us"

I say, "Thanks sarge, you couldn't keep me from going." Luke agreed.

"What's up with Ranger?"

"No word about the dog. We'll find out when he comes in."

We now board the Deuce and all the jovial moods and partying laughter have been washed away. The ride back to the hootch is silent and darkly reflective.

Luker and I get cleaned up and throughout our preparation to head over to the hospital, everybody comes up to us and makes sure we know how they feel. I already know. Pete was one of those guys everybody liked and respected. He was a "class individual." I remembered he was one of the guys that came down to greet us when we arrived here. That was "class."

We get to the hospital and the nurse meets us at the door with the sgt. and lets us in.

"We usually don't allow this but we got the call to expect you. Sgt. Christiano was very close to you guys."

I add, "Nurse, you'll never know." Never seeing her Captain's bars. Sgt. Matlock looks at me and then to the Captain, to apologize, but the Captain nods to him and lets it go.

"This way."

We follow her through the canvassed walled corridor and opens a door that displays a whole ward of men on cots and stretches with all kinds of tubes and strangely sounding machines hooked up. I look around and wipe my face at this "humanity."

"Jesus!"

We finally come up to Pete lying on this stretcher with bloody bandages and blood bottles in his arm. The machine that's beeping continuously shows he's stable.

"That's a very good sign." The nurse says, "But, he's lost a lot of blood."

Luke goes over and says, "Yo, Pete! We're here, buddy!"

Pete opens up his eyes and tries to focus on his visitors. Matlock moves closer and names who's here and where he is. Pete asks who won the Super Bowl?

Matlock says, "Dee! He took all of us with the Jets, but we want a rematch. You want in?"

"Yeah, Pete," I say, trying to break the dark mood.

"I'm going to make it easy for everybody to get their money back. I'm betting the New York Mets to win the 69'World Series, this year."

"I'm with you, Dee! You're on a lucky streak," Pete says, but with obvious pain.

I mention, "Everybody is here but they won't let them in." We're here in spirit for you, buddy. Got anything you want us to do?"

"Yeah, I want you to get my dog, back. He's still up there and he's still alive!"

Matlock says, "WHAT?"

"I'm telling you. He's still alive. They wouldn't go back for him. He was right there by the door as they took off! They wouldn't go back for him. I was screaming and they thought I was nuts but I was looking at him looking at me, as we left. He was just left there!"

We all just looked at each other.

"We had the bastards. They had tried to set up a trap for us but Ranger sniffed it out and we turned it around on them. The guys I was with were good. And, they were pros. We chased those little monkeys all out of their holes and tunnels. We had them in disarray and they were running scared. We were going in for the kill and we were calling in for the air strike, for the mop-up, when we were told to "break off contact"!

We said "What?"

"We had them! They were broken going to quit and command wanted us to break off contact. We were ordered to get back to the LZ coordinates and set up a perimeter defense for extraction. We were getting pulled out and the momentum switched, just like that. The "VC" took advantage of the switch and now they started to cut us up. I couldn't understand it. Everything just fell apart upon the extraction. The copters couldn't land because of the murderous fire and the dense jungle. I get hit and the next thing I know, I'm being placed on a stretcher and being strapped in. I yell for them to get my dog but they say they can't get him in the copter, like this. I'm screaming. I'm strapped in a basket and all I see is my dog running all around looking up at the copter and barking for me to come get him. OH, GOD!"

The hospital monitor shows how much this was taking out of Pete, but the man was crying, for his dog! We all understood, perfectly. And, there was nothing abnormal about it.

I finally blurt out, "Look, Pete, get MAD. You get GODDAMNED MAD! Don't ever forget how mad you are today. And, when you recover from this, you get mad again! Then, you get EVEN. HEAR? For, RANGER! You DON"T GIVE UP! You get better from this, Pete. Our day will come, I promise! Hear Me?"

As we leave, I look at Luker and I say, "I don't think this is the only "fucking," going on around here. "One day the truth will come out." I just hope the people, who are benefiting from all this are still around when that happens.

"Amen, brother." says Luker. Matlock doesn't say anything.

We get Pete's future address for Japan and we leave to go back to the hootch. I hear a radio and the Super Bowl is just "starting." I fall asleep.

That seemed to mark the "turning point." The moment when all hell broke loose on K-9 and a personal vendetta arose between them and us. Up until now it seemed the old superstitions worked, in keeping "Charlie" at bay, from us. But, now, it was apparent they wanted us and wanted us real bad. Rumors came from intelligence and from "other sources" that a higher "bounty" was now placed on K-9's head. The war had just gotten personal between K-9 and the "VC". We played it off, but it had to have a chilling affect on the men. We were also proud to be singled out by them. And, that we had the same effect on them.

PHOTOGRAPHS

King likes his picture taken. Upper right: travel kennel

Lackland AFB War Dog Training Site

Author and King front row, 2nd from left.
Graduating class, Lackland AFB July 1968.

Big B-52 Landing. See corresponding "Bonding" story.

**KC-135 Landing at Base perimeter.
Buddha Mountain in background.**

Walking sentry patrol outside base perimeter in jungle.

The Big "Behemoth" Deuce 1/2

Author and King, a team forever

**Utapao Royal Thai AFB. KC-135 Fuel Tanker landing.
B-52 tail fins below.**

King taking a "break."

U.S. Marine Scout Dog Cemetery
1970 DaNang, RVN
at base of Freedom Hill
3rd MP Battalion, 3rd Marine Division

**"K-9 GRAVEYARD IN MEMORY OF THESE SCOUT DOGS WHO WERE
TRULY MAN'S BEST FRIEND"**

Our dogs loved to fly

lethal cross-hairs

K-9 Posts patroling areas

Pattya Beach—Sac's town by the sea

"incoming!!", shelling our positions

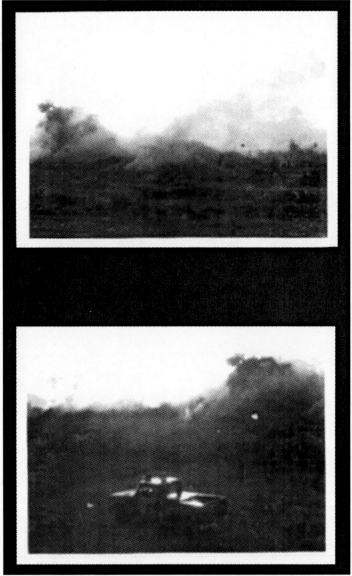

"here they come again!", more shelling our positions

Chapter XVII
IN-COUNTRY

Things really started to happen, now. There was some talk again of dividing up the force to deploy to our air bases in Thailand. Intelligence indicated "Charlie" scurrying up some more trouble there for our B-52's and fighters. That and going on special ops was dwindling our numbers. We also sad to see the first detachment of handlers getting ready to rotate back home.

At this time, it seemed K-9 was losing an average of a dog team a day. All over, reports were coming in of frantic activities by the enemy. Since last year's uprising at "Tet" the Cong seemed to be demoralized and splintered. But, now there was renewal in their tactics and determination. It was going to be interesting to see how we responded. The VC were no doubt getting encouragement and strength by what was going on at home, with all the news of the anti-war demonstrations. We were still in charge here and they knew they couldn't militarily defeat us. But, their strategy seem to be one of demoralization and to hold on long enough to cause a political conclusion to this conflict. It simply came down to a matter of wills and determination. And, we were losing both.

Luker and I were called into the Captain's office. He asked if we thought we could make a trip for him and accompany a task force, to the La Drang Valley region at the "Iron Triangle." The Marines up there were having trouble picking up "Charlie's hiding areas and requested K-9 to help. We very well couldn't say "no," so we just accepted the mission and a five-day pass to Bangkok, "when we get back."

We packed for four days and picked up the dogs at the kennels and loaded the "six pack", a blue six-passenger truck with a cab and flatbed. We headed out to the tarmac where there was a copter waiting for us and took off as soon as we were loaded. They were in a "hurry."

It was a beautiful day with the sun shining but the "Monsoon" season was expected to start pretty soon. I think they wanted this done before "Charlie" had the chance to bury themselves in for the duration.

About an hour later we arrive and land in the middle of this Marine encampment. Must have been about 80 of them along with Vietnamese mountain guides, The Montenyardes. These ancient mountain men knew this land better than "Charlie." And, they were here generations, longer. I get a kick about all the stories I've been hearing from back home about reports of atrocities and pillaging and massacres and rapes, we're supposed to be committing on the population, here. I laugh at this silly propaganda crap and lies and really can't believe our people back home would or could believe it. These Montenyardes guides are living proof to the contrary. If we were really guilty of any of this, it would be these people too we would be fighting. Instead, they see their people being treated fairly and getting food and medicine for their sick. They're working with us and we haven't given them any reason not to. This whole war has boiled down to a tale of double-dealing and double-talking. And, it's coming from both sides. It's unfortunate it's the people who are caught in the "middle."

The Marine Captain comes up to Luker and me and introduces himself, "I'm Captain Robert Ebersole."

There's no insignia markings and no formal saluting, out here, in the field. We know everyone's watching and maybe, so is "Charlie" and you don't want to "mark" the officers, that way, for possible enemy snipers. I laugh when I see that in movies, but in real life, never.

He tells us the information we need to know and gives us a map of the route we're to take and asks if there are any questions. We understand and he wishes us "luck."

"I'm glad you're here with us."

Luke and I smile in acceptance and take a look around.

All eyes are on us as we adjust our gear and get the dogs ready. They know we're to take "point" and for all practical purposes we're now in charge of this mission. It's success or failure will be on our shoulders and their very lives will depend on our decisions and evaluations.

We make sure we have enough water for King and Diablo and then I smile at Luker.

"How'd this happen?" I asked.

"We joined K-9," came the answer.

I bend over to rub King and to wipe his head. I need to get his encouragement. I change "collars" and I whispered to him, "O.K, big guy, let's do this."

King jumps up immediately and let's out a growl. A couple of the marines were getting just a little too close and changed direction, that quickly. I just smiled.

"We'll be O.K!"

With the Captain blowing the whistle all the men stand up and grab their gear. I look at Luke and give him a "thumbs up". I now remove King's muzzle and we start heading out into the jungle. As we take the "point", we move into two single columns, one following me and one following Luker.

Approximately a mile into our "walk", we are to split up but the columns are never supposed to be more than seventy-five yards apart from each other. The Vietnamese mountain men are behind us and they are intrigued seeing how our dogs are working the land for signs of the enemy. We know from intelligence that "Charlie" is here in this valley. They've been using this area for months to strike and then disappear. We're now hoping King and Diablo can pick up something. The estimate is about 100 of them and, again, we know they're here, somewhere.

Just before Luker splits off, I look back and see the men about 30 feet behind me. I look at Luke and we wink to each other. I know we're going to enjoy our "five day pass, R&R" in Bangkok, after this is over.

As Luke splits off to the left I take the right flank. We're to assist each other in case of trouble and we're to cover each other's flank but, right now, I'm out here "all alone" with King.

"Wouldn't have it any other way", I mumble to myself.

"This is really what K-9 is all about," I reason.

I rein in King a little bit and slip him some water from my canteen over my hand. In this humid heat, I pour a little over his head, too.

I watch King's every move intently. Any sign he gives me and I'll get down and give the signal.

"I'll do my job; they just better be able to do theirs." I just hope they are alert enough to see my actions and are paying attention.

After a few minutes, I start feeling strange. As if I'm losing contact with everything. It gets easier to hold the struggling leash but it's as if I can see through the bush. I stop for a second to catch my breath and I can feel my heart racing, a mile a minute. I bend over and pat King on his head for encouragement and he nuzzles my hand and leg with his nose, in return. That's our signal to each other. We're both here, together. No one's leaving.

I realize now I hear no bird sounds and everything is silent. That's when King gets the alert. Unmistakably. I immediately crouch down and signal my position and the "non-visual alert." I want everyone to stop what they're doing and be silent. I don't want any mistakes or giveaways.

I wait and listen. Not a sound, anywhere. I signal I'm going in for a visual and for everybody to stay where they are. I plan to go about ten feet and if still nothing to call up the men ten feet. I do this and yet, still nothing, except I know King has something.

We leave the trail to the right and enter some tall bush. I can even smell it now and it smells bad. I call up the outfit another ten feet and go deeper into the bush.

Very slowly, I'm moving in the direction of an opening of the tall grass. I signal everyone to stay put as me and King approach to this very leafy green tree. It's to this tree that King has led me to but now his head is turning all around in every direction. I'm feeling real bad about this.

I'm about 25 yards off the trail and about the same from the troops. I shake my head as I lift a branch up with my bayonet. It's a cut up old water buffalo with it's stomach all ripped out! Tied up to the tree! It's a TRAP!

I immediately scream, "Get out! get out!, get out!" over the radio. But, I know it's too late.

I turn and try to run in the same direction that I came in but I see three "Charlie" run toward me. They're covered with the blood and the insides of the butchered beast, hanging on the tree. They look like the "living Dead" and very scary. That's how they confused King. They covered their own scent with the buffalo's scent and hide under the bush, allowing King to go after the heavier scent and overlook their positions.

I immediately unhook King for off-leash but I can feel him, as he stays right by my side. He's not going anywhere. I position him around and point him in the opposite direction. I do this so as to not hinder King's deterrence and yet, it allows both him and me more movement. I now turn to confront the three charging "VC." I also now start hearing rapid fire and grenades coming from where the marines are. I feel terrible and awfully mad to have led them into this trap. I now also feel King leave me. But I don't have to know why. I shoot first and one guy falls but the other two are on me, swinging their machetes.

I sidestep one and ram my rifle butt into the second guy's face. Blood comes pulsating out of his nose. It's this pounding contact that now knocks my rifle out of my hands but in one two-step motion I find myself in position to grab the third guy from behind his head and grab his throat. I pull up and over to the right and I hear a "crunch" sound. He immediately gets very heavy and I drop him to the mud.

I look around to see where King is and I see "eternity."

King had jumped two more that were after me and was finishing up as I saw one more now coming at him with a machete up over his head. He was just about to swing down onto King! I was too far away and my rifle was lying on the ground. I was helpless and I was going to see him KILL MY DOG!

I screamed out, NO! He hesitated a fraction of a second. Just enough for this black and silver streak to jump over King and in one unbelievable leap; catch the guy right in his chest. The sword goes one way and his body goes another.

It was DIABLO! And was he PISSED! ! Luke ran over to me as I crumbled to my knees and with tears in my eyes.

"Sorry to take so long, buddy, traffic was bad"! I just looked at him, in no mood to kibitz but I did manage a weak "thank you."

As both dogs come prancing back to where we were, he asks me if I'm OK and I tell him, "I couldn't protect King." King comes into me for his patting. He says, "bullshit."

"You guys just took out six dudes!" "I saw two partners, standing back to back determined to protect each other. And, you did!"

I start praising the big fella, but I know it's only going to get worse.

The firefight was still on as we reached the main element of the task force. I was ashamed of leading these guys into this, but the Captain saw me and "congratulated" me on "extraordinary work." He was just happy to finally get these monkeys out in the open, and get a shot at them.

And it was, "you guys that drove them out. Excellent work!" He now was on the phone to headquarters to give the coordinates of this area. He wanted this whole place "leveled."

As we pull back, the heavy artillery takes over. I thought the world would crack.

When we get back to camp, everybody was jovial and congratulating me and Luker and the dogs. We were given this roast to feast on as we drank some beers. I still felt a little queasy, but it did feel good to live up to the tradition of K-9's reputation. These guys had worked with K-9 before and they knew what to expect from us. Luke and I felt good we didn't fail them. King and Diablo were now resting after their meal.

Chapter XVIII
BANGKOK

I was still a little shook up when our copter landed at Ton Son Nhut. Sgt. Matlock met us immediately and we loaded our equipment and dogs on the "six-pack" for our ride to the kennels. It was good to be home, again. All the hustle and noise. This was more like it!

Word had gotten back and we were congratulated by everyone for the job we did. But, now we were ready for a good five days off. Luke and I were told that there was a transport leaving in two hours for Bangkok, Thailand. If we hurried we could be on it.

After making sure King and Diablo would be ok we jumped into the six-pack, again, and rushed back to the hootch to wash up, pack some things and change clothes. To my delight, all the money I had won on the Super Bowl was there on the light table waiting for me and I was now going to put it to good use. Twenty minutes later, we were out the door and heading back to the tarmac for the two-hour flight to Bangkok.

We landed in Bangkok and hopped into a cab to take us to the "International Hotel." It was the one recommended by Matlock as he had just taken "R&R", himself, and he said this place was ok. A couple of the guys who had been here, also, gave us some pointers on how to maneuver and get around town.

They recommended the first taxi cab driver we liked, to "contract" him to be your personal driver. It would be cheaper that way and you could forget everything else, for the cabbie would know where to go and what to do. It seemed like a good idea to me, so that's what we did. Our driver's name was "Joe." He had done this before with other G.I.'s and said it was "ok" by him.

For the five days, he would charge us two hundred dollars. I said, "too much." We finally agreed to one hundred thirty, but insisted he would take us to his "brother's place," first. We agreed.

"Joe" drove us to the hotel and agreed to come back at six P.M. to pick us up, for the night. Our hotel, from the outside was a reminder of past glory years in regal Bangkok. Although, kept in reasonably good condition, being from New York, it wasn't going to get mixed up with the "Plaza" or the "Waldorf." But, it looked "beautiful" to me, after what we've been through, recently.

I reminded Luke about that rainy night at Camp Bullis during training and how far we've come. He said he couldn't wait to take a "bath."

Luker and I, both, checked in and immediately ordered room service for some sandwiches, cold beer and a bottle of champagne. We went to our rooms on the third floor and took a hot and extremely satisfying bath, anyone could've asked for. When I came out, I took a bite of the sandwich and poured myself a cold beer on ice. As I stood in my air conditioned room, looking at the mirror, I toasted myself, feeling quite good.

"NOBODY was living better than me, at this moment in time."

Luke came in and we congratulated ourselves and started "toasting," everything and everybody and getting real stupid.

Around five-thirty, we went down stairs to meet "Joe." We took a seat in the lobby and surveyed the place, for the first time.

It was getting dark outside, now, and the lights actually made the place looked more elegant than I thought, earlier. It really was a nice place with fluffy white and red curtains and drapes accenting big windows. The walls were papered with gold and black design with small lights placed at strategic locations with room itself centered by a high ceiling with a huge hanging "crystal chandelier." The very picture of one of those scenes I saw in the movies about the Russian commissars, let alone a hotel lobby on the other side of the world.

There were two ceiling fans on either side of the chandelier that kept the lobby very comfortable and the hot stagnant air outside. A door off to the side led to a small cafeteria, I supposed for coffee or tea. On the opposite wall was another door that led to a cocktail lounge and the sounds of a jukebox playing old Frankie Avalon records. I reminded Luke, "That's your Philadelphia homey." He laughed and rolled his eyes, then pointed to "Joe" parking his taxi at the front door. He was five minutes early. I liked that.

As we got into the car, Joe says he's got a great place to go for dinner but I stop him, right off, and says, "It's our first night here and for months I've been wanting a pizza."

Luke says, "Yeah, that sounds good to me, too!"

I always "liked" my man, Luke. We think alike. Joe heads off into the night and we past buildings and structures you would never find in New York.

Buildings with wide, golden-bubbled rooftops and cathedral shaped palaces. No building seemingly higher than maybe ten stories but just built to a different "theme" or texture. However, once we hit the "downtown" district, it all becomes commonly familiar. The hustle and bustle of people shuffling in bunches, dodging traffic and horns blaring, yelling and carrying shopping bags. Some things never change.

"Home", says Luke, and I nod agreement.

A ripe smell hits the open window of the car and ruffles in. I really can't decipher a particular fragrance and I ask Joe, "What's that?"

He says, "That's the canal. Many people live on the canal, in boats called "junks," and do all their cooking there.

We cross this small bridge a most wondrous sight hits us. All these small wooden boats, thousands of them all tied together, it looks like, each with lights and people climbing all throughout the "colony."

"Unbelievable", I murmur to no one in particular.

Dodging other cars and more pedestrians on narrower streets, we finally get to our destination. One we would have never found for ourselves. I can see now how much more convenient and advantageous it is to have this arraignment with Joe.

We get out and Joe says, "# 1 pizza, in town. The Best."

I says, "Good enough, Joe, from here we'll go to your brother's place.

He says, "Good, good, # 1, right here." He points to a black wooden door, next door to the pizza place. "My Brother's place! # 1!"

I look at Luker and we both laugh. "How convenient!"

We open the door to the restaurant and walk up a very narrow staircase. No way could two people maneuver up and down the staircase at the same time. And, yet, that is exactly what happens as we reach about half way up the stairs. The top door opens and with music playing inside this little guy, dressed to the "nines," with an exquisite white three-piece suit and matching hat and very skinny diamond studded tie, comes down the stairs with the most stunningly beautiful girl I've ever seen, in my life. Long straight black hair, she's wearing this body tight red satin dress that's shoulder-less and with a strategic slit up the left/right...er, I don't know which leg, thigh.

As she approaches me, our bodies close together. We're closer than people on a homeward bound rush-hour subway train the day before Christmas. Our eyes lock as our bodies brush up against each other, in the attempt to pass. The scent of her fills me, and, I murmur, "Oh, Dear Jesus," as I immediately form an erection. It has to be the most embarrassing moment.

I feel her hand brush up past my extended member and it seems to pause there for just a moment. We both looked at each other and smile. She then gives me the most sensuous, endearing, heart-stopping expression with both her big dark eyes and her beautiful shaped red lips, slightly open to reveal a most passionate tongue. In a matter of a microsecond, I was "water."

She keeps walking, shaking her long dark hair and most outrageously shaped body, down the stairs, through the door and out of my life.

(A few years from now, there will be song by a singer named Murray Head, "One Night in Bangkok", that will become a favorite. Most people will never fully grasp the meaning of my acknowledging and most appreciative smile I wear every time I will hear that song. Editors note)

When reality returns and normal breathing function resumed, Luke had already reached the top of the stairs and was laughing at me. I must of looked like a, geez, I don't know what, to him. But, I didn't care. I finally reached the top and we entered to sit down to, "Bangkok's No. 1 Pizza!"

The restaurant, itself, seemed like a room right out of the Roaring' twenties. Wooden booths with wooden benches lit by a small electric lamp and covered by a smoke dirty decorative shade with dragons, on each side. A similar wooden wall covered the smoky room and a mirror was on the ceiling. Two slightly moving ceiling fans and festive multi-colored lights also hung on the wall clinging to a small extended border that encircled the whole room, which was painted in red. All things considered, not really that bad! Or maybe it was our festive relaxed mood we were in. Nothing was ever going to be "that bad", in our celebration of life and new experiences.

Luke ordered a couple of beers and I had to go to the "little boy's" room. The window was slit a little and as I dried my hands I took a quick peek outside and amazingly, I saw the girl in the red dress, outside talking with the three-piece suit. They split up and the suit got into a cab, the girl went into the place, next door. Joe's brother's place!

I rush outside and tell Luke.

He says, "Slow down, cowboy!" You know she's gotta be a "paid lady", right?" I look at Luker and I just "look at him."

"How much?" I ask.

"Just figure a lot more than you got. Besides, we got four more days, here, man."

Our beers and "No.1 Pizza" come and we dig in to eat. "Not Bad!" Even with the pineapple and celery sticks. So far, everything's "Not Bad!"

We finish up the pizza and have a few more beers and then decide to hit Joe's brother's place. We pay the check and angle down the skinny stairs, again. No adventure this time. We open the door and hit the breeze on the street. Truly, it has been a "good ride," so far. I now feel like a high-school kid, with his first crush on a "cheerleader." Impossibly, in love, with no chance in hell, with a "paid lady."

"Suppose she's still in there?" I say to Luke.

"Man, get a hold on yourself!" "Walk like a man!" he answers.

I check the time. We told Joe to be back here at 11 P.M. It's already five minutes to ten. "How much trouble can we get into in one hour?"

We straighten ourselves out and open the door. A wave of smoke and music from the record player hits our faces. We enter into a very dark room full of people, talking and laughing. So far, Joe's been on the money. Seems like a good place. We get our eyes "adjusted to the dark," which now sounds faintly familiar, and walk down three steps and amble over to the bar.

The bar is all in red. Red walls, red drapes and red lights, affixed to the counter. Red lights shining from the ceiling and for a change of pace, red rugs, on the floor. I kind of like it, but Luker whispers to me "Mafia."

I just nod.

"We're here, now. We got to have one drink.

We order two beers and I search the crowd for my "little Red Riding Hood."

"Red" must be the favorite color in Thailand, I says to Luke.

He grins and then nudges me to look over at the corner of the bar.

"You really have to admit it. The Oriental woman are outrageously attractive and sexy," I say.

Luke can't hear me, as he is busy playing his own "eye games" with this woman about twenty feet from us. I can see this is going to be one of those nights.

Here we are. Two eighteen year olds. First time away from home, halfway around the world, in a city historically labeled as "Sin City" since biblical days.

"If they could only see me now", I smile.

A mid size pudgy man wearing an immaculate white three piece suit, walks up to us and introduces himself.

"Sowardee, you must be Dee and Luker. Welcome! My name is Sak and I own this place. "Joe" told me he was bringing you tonight I hope you like the show. Make yourself comfortable. Please"

I graciously, thank him for his hospitality.

"Where are you from in the States?"

"I'm from New York, Luke, here is from Philadelphia."

I nudge Luke, but he's already talking with the "eye" girl.

"He's knows how to enjoy himself." Sak laughs.

"That is good." Sak motions to the bartender and the man brings us over two more beers.

I say, "Thank you. Allow me to buy you one, back"

He nods his consent and for the bartender to bring him over a liquid in a rock glass. We toast each other and smile. I like this guy. He has style. Also, someone I feel may be good to know. I then see "little red riding hood" exiting the lady's room.

I say to Sak, we will be in Bangkok for only a few days but, if there's anything I can do to repay your hospitality, please don't hesitate to ask.

"Ha! Dee. Maybe if this were New York. But, this is my town. I like you. You do the right thing. Now you go and see your lady. You can see Sak, anytime."

I look at Sak in amazement, but I can see he means it so I bow to him and approach my lady in red.

As we approach each other our eyes never waver. We stare at each other for a long time without speaking. She then smiles slyly as she says her name is "Nancy" in a very thick Oriental dialect, "Nancy," I say. "No way!"

She laughs and says, "Yes. For you, I want to be Nancy."

As we're talking I can feel her right hand rubbing up and around my thigh and leg. A most magnificent sensation wells up inside of me and in no time I'm advertising my emotions very "outstandingly", again.

"Magnificent." she utters softly into my ear, now as the music begins to play and the people head back to their seats. I grab "Nancy's" hand and lead her over to the bar where Luker and "eyes" are getting "stupid." I rap Luker on his ass and tell him, "Let's get out of here."

Luker looks up, finally, and sees "Little Red…" and I finish "Nancy."

Luke, says, "Nancy."

I say, "Yeah, Nancy."

Luke says, "I want you to meet "Alice.""

"Alice?"

We both crack up hysterically as we move towards the door. I past Sak and greet him as we leave, everyone laughing. Joe is outside, and he is laughing, too!

I wake up the next morning and she was gone. Not a trace was left to remind me of one of the most memorable nights of my life. I immediately snap to full wakefulness and throw the covers off the bed. My clothes are scattered all over the room signaling all the eventful stops in our oblivious sexual journey from the door to the bed, scant few hours before. In actuality, it was only a five-step approach. It just didn't seem that way last night with the both of us pawing, kissing, biting and scratching each other's clothes off.

I look and my keys and wallet are on the night table next to the container with the melted ice and half drank drinks.

I grab my pants and put them on and call the desk, downstairs. My hands come up with all my money from in my pockets as I wait for the attendant to answer. I rub my face and sit back down on the bed, trying to take in the whole adventure, and "Nancy."

"She left about 6A.M., sir. She got into a cab. Is everything alright?"

"Fine, It's OK," I say as I check my watch, which shows 9:30A.M.

"Thank you, would you connect me to room #322, please."

The phone rings and I hear Luker pick up the phone.

"YEAH, who the hell is this?"

"Ho Chi Mihn, asshole. Me, what's up?"

"Me, forchristsake! A second ago, anyway."

"You know, youse guys from Philly are known to be Anni-males!"

"Call me, later." Well, at least, I know Luke is OK, anyway.

I jump into the bathroom and take a shower. As I'm shaking last night out of my head and letting the warm water take over my body and senses, I see all these "hickey" marks, all over my chest and back. I look like a swarm of "Man Eating Nancy's" attacked me.

"And, they're the worse kind because you can never forget them once they leave their mark on you!"

I got to find her and the only place I know to look is at "Sak's Place."

I get out of the shower and start putting on some clothes, when my phone rings. I think its Luker.

"Yeah, Luke, How about some breakfast?" When a soft voice answers, "I can't but how about Lunch?"

"Nancy? Is that you?" Where are you?"

"I'm sorry, I had to leave. But, I do want to see you, again. How about, later about six, at Sak's?"

"You read my mind, girl. I'll be there."

"Good, I can't wait," and she hangs up.

I call for Joe and ask him to meet me at the hotel "about noon." I then slipped a note under Luker's door with a "Do not disturb" sign, on it, and go downstairs for some breakfast.

On my way to the lounge I stop at the desk and ask the guy there when he started work, today?

"I started 12, Midnight, last night, sir."

I asked, "Then you saw my party come in last night and the lady leave, this morning?"

"Yes, sir!"

"By chance, have you ever seen her, before?"

"No, sir, very beautiful, # 1 Sir!"

"And, when she left, did she say anything?"

"No, sir, but her face showed she had a 'good time."

"Yes, sir, GOOD TIME."

I nodded "Thank You!" And, I went in the cafeteria lounge for some coffee.

I picked up an English printed newspaper and read the story about the "VC" bombing Saigon and Ton Son Nhut, AGAIN! Geez, I didn't even know they did it the FIRST time. I felt kind of queasy that here we are enjoying ourselves and everyone else is catching hell, back home. And, King! How's he doing? I bet he's wondering where I am!

I try to get my mind off it a second and read the sports. They're just starting to play baseball spring training. I'm glad the world hasn't gone COMPLETELY insane, yet! I think back to all my people I have home in New York and wonder what's going on in their lives. Most of them are still in school and "debating" this mayhem. Here, I am in Bangkok. Living it! A place where most people only read about in novels!

I now become aware of these two older men with European accents, having breakfast at the table next to me. They're discussing Viet Nam and I eavesdrop to listen to the discussion. The first man is an older man, of the two. A simple and unassuming man. But, I sense a quality of pride and humble nobility, about him. He has wisdom maybe for the ages wearing an old fashion suit with a vest. He says, simply, "it's bad." He doesn't blame the people as much as he blames the governments He goes on by saying that people should be allowed to choose whatever it is to be their destiny.

"What does simple farmers and peasants know about Democracy or Communism? And, Why do these people, who work their lives away in rice plantations and mud fields, need with Cadillac's and TV's?"

"They only worry about what they know, farming and the weather for irrigation."

"But, what about their leaders?" I interrupt.

"What leaders?" he challenges. "I don't care who is in charge as long as they leave me alone with my land."

"My friends, they understand me. A man's word is his legacy. That will be all he will ever have in this life. Governments come and go but it is the people that will always remain."

"Governments have no 'word' or loyalty, only people have that and it is only the people that get to suffer and get hurt, not the government."

I actually understood and agreed with what he meant and I added, "Then it's the people that should rise over the government or at least be willing to "direct" it."

"Yes, my friend, for only the people suffer if they don't."

"People must wake up to their responsibilities to direct their destiny, not let government do it for them. No government can."

So, now I understood, what has been bothering me, ever since Pete's tragedy.

I'm the one fighting, but because of this stinking situation, brought on by irresponsible management in governing. We're the one's who suffer. Not the people who caused this. What a total sham! And, yet, it is the people's fault, also, for putting these people into their positions of power and allowing it to happen.

And for what? So "glory" can be ascertained? "Money" can be made? "Power" can be exerted?

I see Luker get off the elevator with "Alice" and walk her to the cabstand, outside the front door. She gets in after one long kiss and rides away. He now comes in and sees me having some coffee and sits down at the table.

"Well if it isn't the bowlegged buckaroo!" I say.

"Oh, man. Shut-up I don't want to hear it."

I show him the paper.

"Shit! So we go back?"

"Yeah, I guess. Joe will be here in a few minutes. Let's go over to the base and see what the situation is, over there, for transportation, back. Before we do, however, I want to do a little shopping, first.

Joe pulls up at 12 on the dot. Good man, Joe. We got lucky when we found him.

We get into the cab and I ask him, "If I want to get Sak a present for his generosity last night, Joe What would you recommend?"

"Oh, he loves Havana Cigars. And, he drinks his Cognac. He is partial to Amaretto, too!"

"Ok, let's get him some CEE-gars and Amaretto then."

I give Joe a hundred dollars and he drives us to the airbase. He then goes on his "shopping spree" for us.

Luker and I go over to base ops and after showing him our I.D. cards, I ask the Sgt. there if there is anything going back to Saigon. He says a C-130 cargo is leaving at 11:37P.M. tonight. I look at Luke and he begrudgingly says, "Yeah, let's do it!"

I say "OK."

The Sgt. says, "Get here by nine, that's twenty-one hundred hours, for confirmation."

I thank him and then we head over to the Exchange. I've never used my ration card since I don't smoke cigarettes or drink liquor, but now I want to get some for Sak and for Joe. We load up on a few bottles of this and a few bottles of that and load it in a shopping cart and head back toward the front gate. Joe is back already from his purchases and we get in the car and head back to the hotel.

Looking out the window of the traveling taxi, he says, "A storm is on its way."

Looking at each other, we acknowledge and Luker says, "Yeah! We know"

The radio is on and we hear our new President, Richard M. Nixon giving a speech.

Chapter XIX
"RANGER"

"We cannot assert that a policy of sustained reprisal will succeed in changing the course of the contest in Viet Nam. What we can say is that even if it fails, the policy will be worth it.

Excerpts from Memo:

McGeorge Bundy assistant and advisor to President Lyndon B. Johnson
February 7, 1965

We arrive back at the hotel and I ask Joe if he would wait for us. It's now 4:45P.M. I want to be at Sak's for my six o'clock date with Nancy. I promise Joe it will be an "early night," for him. He says, "ok" and pulls over to the parking area to wait for us.

"Thanks, Joe, we'll be back in 45 minutes", I say.

I go over to the front desk and ask for the manager. The clerk says, he's not there but can he be of service? I explain our orders have been changed and that we'll have to sign out of our rooms as soon as we can get packed. He asked if everything was satisfactory.

"Too satisfactory, we really didn't want to leave. I'm sure we'll be back, again."

The clerk says, "No problem, I'll have your bill ready when you are ready."

I acknowledge and thank him for his understanding.

In a few minutes, we pack and come down with our bags, now wearing our field fatigues to sign out. It's 5:30P.M. as we get in the taxi, it begins to drizzle. I tell Joe to go to Sak's and to wait for us. It gets closer to six o'clock and the night begins to take effect.

The city's lights have a hypnotic effect on the casual. It's moody and seems unaffected by the tension cast down by the atmosphere surrounding it.

Equally unaffected, Joe's cab whizzes and careens through the ancient capitol's narrow, foreign streets, oblivious to it's traffic. We pull up in front of Sak's club as the rain begins to come down harder.

We dash into the nearly empty club, with the jukebox playing and immediately see "Nancy," standing at the bar. She sees my uniform and her disappointment etched across her face.

"You had to know I would leave in a couple of days, didn't you?"

"Yes, but I didn't think it was going to be so soon. Will I ever see you again?"

Hesitatingly I respond, "I'd like to think so, but I don't know."

She turns her face toward to jukebox. "I hate this war."

She's either the "world's greatest actress" or she really is hurting to see me going back.

"I really don't know what to say."

"Don't say anything."

I surprise myself at my determination at the lousy situation. We kiss.

Sak now comes up, "Leaving so soon?"

"Yes, I have a real good friend that's waiting for me. But I would like to feel comfortable in possibly contacting you, someday, if I may, sir."

"Dee, call upon me anytime you can my friend. Joe is a real good judge of people. And, he likes you guys."

I shake his hand and say "Thank you! I think that just might happen!"

We go out to Joe's taxi and unload our "presents" for Sak. He is genuinely touched and holds my hand, again.

"Please take care of yourselves, my friends. I truly will wait to see you again." I look at "Nancy" one more time. No words, but I knew, no words were necessary.

"Get us to the airbase, Joe!"

The traffic as in all big cities is all a mess as the rain starts affecting the wet roads. Luke wonders if the rain will delay our flight.

When we get to the main gate entrance, we get out with our bags. It's now eight-thirty two P.M.

"We got a little something for you too, partner. You take care, Joe."

Joe gives me a card with a phone number on it.

"Just in case you ever get back to us."

We run through the puddles over to base cps to sign in.

Luke says, "Hey, we really do have some friends, now, don't we?"

"I hope so! It just might be that we'll need all the "friends," we can get, someday."

"I think I have an idea of what you're planning, Dee. And, I think it's crazy. But, count me in. Don't even think about forgetting that."

"I won't and I wouldn't WANT to, buddy."

The two-hour flight passes quickly as we both have a lot on our minds and to deal with. None of which is good. But, I can't believe the changes in me since I volunteered for k-9. So many things have happened since then.

As the alarm goes off for landing, we strap ourselves in our places. It will feel good to be with King, again. I know we did the right thing by coming back sooner than was expected.

The big plane touches down and rolls to a stop. A minute later the doors open and for the first time we see small fires and destroyed areas, having been hit by a barrage of mortar fire, the continuous rain having very little affect on them. It's about 2:30A.M. I know everybody is at the kennels.

We grab a passing jeep and hitch a ride. The guy was good enough to take us straight to the kennels. No damage or fires, here, thank God.

Matlock is at his desk as we walk in.

"What the hell..."

Luker tells him that the papers in Bangkok said, "You guys couldn't live without us."

"Thanks for coming back. I hate to admit it but we really can use you two. It's been pretty wild here, lately. We've had some guys take some hits."

"A cute little ditty, from intelligence seems to have "Charlie" raising the bounty on our heads, again. They'll pay big for proof of a kill, like a dog's ear or even a unit patch."

"Hell," says Luke," I'll give them $250, to leave me alone."

"It hasn't been pretty, around here." says the sarge, ignoring Luker. "They're really targeting the kennels, now, and K-9 in particular."

"Put us on the roster for tomorrow", as I go to check buddy.

"They're good but they'll be glad to see you guys." Matlock says, smiling.

"I don't know why!"

We go out the door to the back and see that both King and Diablo are up and wide awake. They must have heard our voices. Their wagging tails of greetings is worth a thousand nights in Bangkok. As we approach, King is straining at the leash, prances a few steps coming to me, takes a swig of water, then comes to me, again, in between, stretching his two front paws and wagging his tail. It's a self-styled uninhibited frenzy and it's the best kind of welcome anybody could ask for.

"I'm glad to see you guys, again," the lieutenant says, coming out of his office.

"We're really starting to mount up the stats, lately."

"Good morning, Sir, that's why we got back here. How bad is it?"

"Well, since the bounty, country-wide, we're averaging about a dog-team and a half, a day, for the last month and a half. All reports are coming in to a situation that can't last if we're to be effective to do this job."

"What about new replacements or people from the states."

"We're going around asking for OJT transfers, now. But, not too many want this kind of job. They'll be no one from home until as least September at the earliest and it's been discussed..."

We both notice the pause/hesitancy in the lieutenant's response and look at each other, "We may initiate RVN soldiers to cross-train over."

"What?"

"Listen," the Lt. continues, "they'll eventually have to be trained, sooner or later. We all know that's coming. It might as well be now."

I turn my head and look at King and my eyes fill with tears, and disgust.

"Enough of this bullshit." I murmur, under my breath.

Luker picks up my mumbling and starts to smile. The Lieutenant looks at us, I'm enraged and tearful and Luker is smiling.

"You guys are nuts, how do you guys get along, so well?"

I tell him, "We compliment each other so well. With us, you get the complete package."

Luker then chimes in about how Pappy ever got to be the way he is, with his "mumbling".

We hear the phone ring in the hootch and Sgt. Matlock picks up the phone. A few minutes later he's calling for the Lieutenant.

Luke and I now start rubbing up the dogs a bit and talk with them a little.

"How would you guys like to see Bangkok, one day?" Luker starts asking Diablo. I start feeling better.

The Sgt. now calls us from the hootch.

"We got a call from the main gate. I don't know why, but, they're asking for us to send someone over there to help them with a situation."

"Do we need to take our dogs?" I ask.

"No." says the Lt. "I'll be going with you, too. This sounds too incredible."

"We'll take the six-pack and, Sgt, call the doctor. Have him meet us at the infirmary and advise him of this. immediately"

We start heading to the main-gate, on the other side of the base. The rain finally starts to let up into a fine mist. It never completely ever stops but it comes to a point where you don't feel it, or you're so busy to realize it.

We pull up to the gates. The big spotlights and the guardhouse with the wire fence-gate are working and we see the two guards and their supervisor off to the side of the gate.

A crowd of people had gathered around both inside and outside the fence. Everyone seems to be standing around a clump of rags, or something. Whatever it was, it was filthy and wet and next to dead. At first I thought it was a man, then, as we got closer, I could distinguish a tail and a dog's head. We all looked at one another.

"Sorry to bother you guys." says the gate guard. "We sometimes get strays walk up to the gate but, well, this one is different. Are you guys, MISSING a dog?" The Lieutenant goes over to the poor creature and tries to inspect the half-dead dog's leather collar, which he is still wearing. The dirt and mud and insects are caked on the belt. I bring over some water and a rag. The rag is for the Lieutenant; the water is for the dog. The dog's tail is still defiantly wagging.

I say, "God Bless, this dog's got a lot of spunk and fight still in him. He's a credit to himself. Never saying "never".

I lift his head and he sips at the water.

"Amen," says one of the guards.

"Let me have a little light, here", says the Lieutenant, switching on his penlight.

"Ranger!"

"HOLY SHIT!! RANGER!" just realizing his own words.

I almost drop his head in my astonishment.

"Jesus, GOOD, LORD!! RANGER!"

The guard supervisor asks, "What's a Ranger?"

"This is Pete's Dog! I yell! OHMIGOD!!"

Luker immediately gets on the radio and Tells Matlock, up at the kennels. He also tells him to have that doctor ready at the infirmary.

"We'll be there in two minutes!"

We hear Matlock, now screaming on the radio, "Where's that doctor? He's needed, urgently in one minute … and I mean NOW! MISTER!"

"Take it easy big guy. We'll do the rest for you."

We get a blanket from the gatehouse and gently slip it under the emaciated dog. Lieutenant and I slowly and gently lift him up and put him on the back seat of the six-pack. The Lieutenant tells Luke, "Get us there."

"I'll go with security, if I can, sir." I say, "We'll give you a red light escort to the infirmary.

On the way to the hospital, I explain what this is all about to the now arriving security supervisor. He's the same one that remembers the "Bob Hope" caper and says so, to me, smiling. He shakes my hand, acknowledging, he knows the truth about that situation. But now, he says, shaking his head, "My GOD! You say, four weeks!"

"We'll just have to pull this dog through. Nothing else will do for this hero!"

I like this guy. Again, it's shown to me we have the men here to finish this war. We have some very good people here. There are no "assholes", here, as either they are being thought of or worse, back home. Most are only hard-working loyal standup kind of men who love their country. I can't understand why we are in such a quagmire of a situation, here. It's almost like we're not being ALLOWED to win!

It's unbelievable how much activity is going on at 3:45A.M. The flashing red light does come in handy, in a few spots but, eventually, we get to the infirmary.

Two guys, dressed in white, but not doctors, from what I can figure, meet us at the entrance of the tent like structure, half canvas and half brick.

"Just like the military to just do things half way", I murmur.

They wheel their stretcher to where told and gently we all lift Ranger out of the six-pack.

"This is a dog!" I don't understand." says one of them. I was told this was a priority-one emergency".

"This is Captain McNeil soldier. You got a "hero" on that stretcher. Is the doctor in there?"

"Yes, sir, He just arrived a few minutes ago and he's in the scrub room."

"Thank you, son, now get this hero inside, A.S.A.P."

Blood is seen on the back seat. "He's in a pretty bad situation." And, we all acknowledge it.

"He'll pull through, with what he just did, he's got to."

"Besides," said Liker, "He's got a date with a certain crew chief from that helicopter, that pulled out on him."

"And, then to Bangkok, too!" I murmur.

"That can happen, too," murmurs Luker, back.

I ask permission from the Lieutenant and, given the "ok," I ask the Captain, "Sir, would it be possible to get a line to Japan and call Pete, about Ranger? It's his dog."

"I don't see why not, but, let's wait until morning and see how this comes out, first." I begin to think that this guy's a "good man." Too good for all this crap!

We're all still at the hospital as the morning shift start to arrive for their tour of duty. The clock on the wall says 7:40A.M. as I get up from my stretched-out position to see about getting a cup of coffee. This is the second time I'm here and I'm not crazy about it. Never did like hospitals but, I guess they're really a necessary. I give my utmost respect for these people who work here and do what they do, always being around the sick and wounded and hardly hearing a cheerful word. I know I could never do what they do. These women and men are true heroes to the fullest definition of the word, with their dedication and commitment. They are just another example of the kind of people who came to the call of their country. Our country should be proud of its sons and daughters. And, their dogs, too!

I ask a nurse if there was a chance to get a couple of cups of coffee. She asked, "Who I was there to see" and I mention the K-9 dog. She didn't say a word. She just spun around and went into the inner ward. Two seconds later she returned with two steaming cups.

"I'm sorry, I don't have any sugar or cream."

"I've learned to like it just like this, Thank You!"

"No, Thank you! For what you guys do! You have to be either crazy or the bravest people I know, to be out there, in the jungle, like that!"

"Actually, it's pretty nice, once you get used to it. But, you know, that's funny, because that's what I say about your job."

"Susan."

"Hello, Susan…. John."

"I'm sorry, you should be an officer. Correct?"

"Yes, Second Lieutenant by an Act of Congress and two years in nursing school."

I smile, "You do a good job. I'm going back to my partner back there, but, if anything comes out..."

"Don't worry, I'll come and get you."

"Sounds like a plan to me, a NICE plan." I smile and return to Luke. Still "resting", I kick his shoes and he says, "I'm awake, god dammit! What time is it?"

It's about an hour later, 8:30A.M. The door opens. About ten of the other handlers walk in. The Captain and the Lieutenant is with them. I report, "Nothing yet, but it should be soon."

Sgt. Matlock says, "You've got to give this doctor some credit. He's really fighting for "Ranger."

"Yeah," Ike says, "Well, Ranger did alright, too!"

I think that sometime it's a double "whammy" to be as "tight" as we are. It's great for the togetherness but when a disaster happens, as it occasionally does, it's catastrophic on all of us.

"When you want to make that call, it's all hooked up." The captain says. "You can make it from here."

It turns 10 a.m. and no one has left. We're just sitting around and I wonder how ol' Parker is doing up at Pleiku. A card game would be good, now, to distract the heavy atmosphere. Haven't really kept in touch with anybody since we got here and except for the accidental "bumping" into someone, on one of our excursions or the momentary intelligence report, no one knows how the others are doing.

It's at that moment the doors burst open and Susan rushes up to us, sitting around the canvassed wall waiting room. "John, oh forgive me, Captain!" Go on, Lieutenant "Sir, Ranger, is going to be OK!"

"YES!" Everybody starts hugging each other and congratulating themselves.

"That's great news, Lieutenant. Who assisted in the procedure?"

"Captain Mallory, sir, He was on the phone, during most of it, with the surgeon-veterinarians in Japan. It was unbelievable to see something like that."

"Well that's one dog too good for "Charlie" to get!" says Sgt. Matlock.

"You can say that again," says Luker as he eyes me.

"Sir, about that phone call? I know of a certain little guy from Bayonne who would love to here this!"

"Go ahead, soldier."

"I'll show him the way, sir." Susan says.

As we walk down the corridor, I hear a "little chatter," but, seriously, I can only think about how happy Pete is going to be. In another world, Susan, would be a lady any man would test himself for.

Wearing very little make-up and dressed in army fatigues, with her sleeves rolled up, her femininity is very apparent. At approximately 5 ft. 5in.and her brown hair tied in a bun under her cap, she certainly didn't have to prove anything to anybody. Susan could have given any of those girls, on stage with Bob Hope, a run for their money, in my opinion. But, I've chosen my course of action with the ladies, a long time ago. With everything so unpredictable, I just couldn't get involved with someone, now. It was bad enough to have all my memories of home. I've already seen how a moment of hesitation could be the difference between life and death.   I need my mind crystal clear and concentrating on the situation at hand for King and I to get through this. I can't be worrying about someone else or a situation I had no control over.

We walk over to the desk and she indicates to pick up the phone. Captain Mallory has come out of the surgical room and is being congratulated and applauded by the others. I look at Susan, who hasn't left my side and I squeeze her hand, for "Thanks." She smiles and squeezes back. Soon the hook-up is in place and I hear the nurse telling an orderly to wheel the bed right to the phone.

"Hello?" a weak and hesitant voice says.

"Is there a way to get this over the intercom?" I ask Susan.

She immediately goes behind the desk and a "squelch" comes over the speakers in the corridor.

"Pete, this is John. Have we got some news for you, buddy. Everyone's here, too!"

"John what have you guys done now?"

"Pete, we're on live and we need to keep our trade secrets, buddy."

"Captain McNeal is here and he's got something to tell you."

"Sgt. Christiano, Pete, how are you, son?"

"Fine, sir, a little weak, but I'm Ok. Except for my dog."

"Well soldier, maybe we can do something about that, too! We're all standing here in the infirmary because a true soldier and a friend of yours just walked in a few hours ago, looking for you. He's going to be fine. I've got Captain Mallory's word on it."

There is nothing, but silence.

"Did you hear me, son?"

"He heard you, Captain", Matlock says. We can now all hear Pete crying on the other end.

I look at Susan and she turns the intercom off. The other guys silently started to leave. Not in despair or disappointment but rather with a new pride and determination to get this job done with no apologies.

I still had Pete on the line, for another second or so, and I tell him, before the line goes dead, "I've got an idea, Pete. You get well and me and Luke will keep in touch." Don't give up, buddy!"

"Yeah, and you guys, too!"

CLICK!

Susan looks at me. Her eyes are red. She is a very special person. I tell her "Thank you for everything."

"Err.... would it be alright if we could come by to see Ranger, once in a while. While, he's recuperating?"

She says, "You better, but only on days."

I say that's great since we work nights.

"What's your dog's name?"

"King. He's a good dog!"

She says, "He'd better be!

Chapter XX
"JIM MORRISON"

"We think it plausible that effective and sustained reprisals, even in a low key, would have a sustained depressing effect upon the morale of Viet Cong cadres in South Viet Nam.

Excerpts from Memo:
McGeorge Bundy to President Lyndon B. Johnson
February 7, 1965

The next few days are spent trying to keep dry as the "Monsoons" take full effect. "Charlie"´ even seemed to capitulate to nature's wraith as only a few mortar rounds found their way to targets on the sprawling airbase. Intelligence kept up a steady endless stream of enemy movement in the An Khe Valley and up north, but we didn't experience a noticeable increase in confrontations, just a steady harassment, but no direct confrontation.

In this kind of psychological warfare it had always been thought the enemy would have to carry it's supplies and we have always respected their ability to live off the land or survive with just the necessities, with never a wasteful thought, in how impractical the circumstances allowed. I had always wondered what "Charlie" would have done if it had "three days" in our garbage dump, with all that we disregard or throw away. They could probably build a new city. But, now, combining the dense heat with the rain, washing out roads and whole landscapes of the terrain mandating the resurgence of the vegetation in the jungle, it had to affect anything human.

Add that to the fact that this region was home to over 2,000 types of lizards and snakes, it's no wonder that even the fighting has to take a temporary second place to mere survival. Yet, it was obvious "Charlie" was up to something.

We were getting many requests for our dog teams from units, all over the area, now, and, I was "temping" with the 1st. Air Cavalry riding around impenetrable areas in helicopters were breath-taking and King seemed to enjoy the rides.

We were to go in and recon an area about 50 miles out. It was kind of unsettling to know that "Charlie" was there but how serene everything was from above. There was just a steady popping or "pinging" in our ears. I asked one of the team what kind of bug made that kind of sound? He laughed and asked the team leader, "What was the name of the "bug" making that noise?" The leader turned around to meet my question and said, "Charliesniperitus."

The whole team laughed and I didn't get it. The guy next to me pointed to a hole in the side of the copter.

"That hole wasn't there a few minutes ago."

"What?" I said, just as another one materialized next to it.

"Holy Shit!" I said.

"Yeah, that's a bullet hole coming from "Charlie" down below. Not much protection in these 'taxis', just basic transportation. That "pinging" sounds are rounds rattling around this tin can."

The signal and the light for our imminent landing came back to us and we all jump off the 'copter in precision timing. We immediately headed for the cover of a large growth of grass the team leader points out as the big bird takes off mere seconds later.

There was to be no more talking, now. We had a job to do using just hand signals. The sun was out which only made the land feel like a steam bath. We used some black cover-up on our hands, faces and arms to deflect the sunlight off our skin. It was strange to be working, again, in the daylight, but it was essential to get "Charlie's" activities reported and the reasons back to base. And it was considered an advantage in using K-9 for their sense of smell and hearing, on these patrols.

We weren't out too long before King detected something in the wind and lifted his head high and to the right of our position. I immediately stopped and crouched down holding up my left hand up and in a fist, over my head. The team, approximately 10 yards behind my lead, immediately stopped and headed off the small trail and covered up. As I looked back, I only saw the team leader and heard nothing. I liked working with these guys. They were very professional. He was to relay whatever signal I sent to him to the rest of the six-man team. I pointed off to left and formed a circle with my hand to signify "alert", "non-visual." It's the leader's job never to lose sight of me and always be in visual contact with the rest of the team.

As I head as quietly as I can further into the bush, the leader now occupies my spot and waits. I try to move silently and the wet grass absorbs as much sound as it can, in compliance. About 25 feet we come to a clearing and I call up the leader.

Even though I have him on a very short leash the team leader stays a few feet from me, respecting King. I point out the clearing and it's the big freshly dug mound that King keeps looking at that captures our attention. The perception is from here is that it was meant that no one would have detected this searching from the air, with all the wet jungle coverings hiding the land's bulging shape or recent activity. As a matter of fact it would probably be next to impossible to detect this anywhere but from the way we came.

At first it looked like maybe it was an entrance to a "VC" tunnel or cavern, we keep hearing about in this area. Signaling back to our back-up team, we both moved in to take a closer look when King immediately stops cold in his tracks. I try to urge him to go on, but he won't move an inch. I stay right behind him and order the leader, "Don't move"!

This is King's alert for booby-trap. I'm looking all around and then finally see a very thin, almost invisible wire crossing over the path we're on. I'm sweating and taking very short breathes, but one more step from either of us and we'd all be blown away.

I point and the leader says, "Stay here, I'll take care of this."

I stay exactly where I am and put King in a "down position." But, I can see he's fidgety and uncharacteristically excited. I don't like this. I can now hear the other men getting into position behind me.

Slowly crawling to the edge of the clump of grass and leaves, the leader takes a long time observing everything and finally I see him snip three blades of grass and then slowly lifts up a "trap door" type covering from the bulge of grass and leaves. Two fragmentation grenades are lifted out and put on the side. He now peers inside the pit for the first time and then slowly closes the "door." He ambles back to us and tells his men that we found a cache of food and weapons, along with some clothes. He realizes that this is what "Charlie" is doing all around the countryside in they're "movements." They're storing up supplies in strategic areas and to have them for a later date, when they come back. From what I can see there' s enough in there to restock up to possibly 30 men.

"THAT'S IT! That can change the whole outcome of this thing. If we can break up their supply caches, no matter how many men they have, they're finished!"

He immediately gets on the radio and signals his exact position. He asks for permission to destroy this cache and survey the surrounding area for any more "storage areas." The reply was startling. We were to withdraw immediately and head back to the pre designated "L-Z' '(Landing Zone). The leader asks for confirmation. As all this is happening I'm watching King.

He's acting very agitated and getting harder to control. There can be only one reason for that and we're not in any situation for it. I tell the leader to let's get out of here, NOW! But he tells me, "We got to destroy this thing. You guys take off for the L-Z, I going to light this place up."

The clouds are turning to an ominous shade of gray as late afternoon approaches. We find the small trail that led us in to this place and we now start to run for our pick-up. Two quick explosions come from where we had just been and we can see the smoke rising into the clouds. But now, the sound of small gunfire fills the air behind us.

Two-guys immediately drop off and form a protective screen for the rest of us and probably to cover the leader as he rushes up to meet us. I'm only praying that the "Huey" will be there to pick us up.

Another 50 feet, or so, 2 more guys drop off and take up positions on either side of the trail to give support for the others when they reach them. Judging by the sounds of the shooting, the action is getting closer and all we're doing is leading "Charlie" to the L-Z. Not a very practical or bright maneuver.

Heavy equipment explosions start tearing up an area about a mile from where we're going. That's standard procedure for extractions. It serves two purposes. The first is to "advertise" the wrong landing zone for the extractment to the enemy and the second is the subtle way of telling the team that the copter is on it's way and to get to the extraction point, NOW!

We're still about 100 yards from the L-Z and the shooting is getting heavier from all points.

"King, my boy, this Sucks!" He nudges my hand in agreement as we stop for the others to catch up. As they do, I see that two are hit and bleeding.

"Com'mon." the leader says to his men.

Running the path together, he tells me, "Can you believe Central never gave me permission to blow the cache? I hope they don't get mad at me."

We get to the outskirts of the L-Z and "Charlie"snipers are all over us. Finally, we hear the "Whoop-whoop-whoop" sound of the chopper coming in for us. There is not a friendlier sound to come out of heaven. We hear radio contact but the firefight is raging high as "Charlie" is really "pissed-off" at us for blowing up their stuff.

I let King go "off leash", but I tell him to stay with me, which he does. It's the only way I can help get the two wounded to the copter. We get over to the copter and another man goes down. He gets scooped up by another and heads behind me for the extraction.

Chaos is out of control! Everything is coming to a boiling point as the chopper drops even lower to get us. The wind and the sound of the engines is actually drowning out the shooting but I can still hear those "ping-ping bugs," again, all around me. As I turn around, I see the team leader go down. The last guy runs over and picks him up and heads for us. The chopper starts to emit a strange sound and from about the 50 feet she is from us I can see she's in trouble. I stop and call King to "Heel" and "get down!" Then, right in front of us the chopper goes into a dive and hits the ground. I immediately run for cover in the bush, King right beside me.

I'm still holding on to the two wounded soldiers and keep King with me and from attacking the enemy.

"If only these little bastards would come out and show themselves," I utter to myself.

As if to please me and satisfy my wish, I finally see them coming out into the clearing. There are only about eight of them. We must have done better than we thought. They were attacking the team leader and the last three members that were still standing. I put the two guys I had, down, and called King to my side.

"Let's go, big guy."

And then, at the very top of my lungs, I let out this yell. I always did this seeing it done so many times in the movies and when I played soldier or cowboys and Indians, when I was a kid. "YEEEEEEEEEOOOOOOOOWWWWWWWWW!!"

I don't know why. It seemed appropriate and it always summoned up all my courage. This time, however, all it did was to put everyone's attention on to me. And, as I was still about ten yards from anybody, it wasn't a very "good idea."

Three of the enemy immediately started running towards me with swords. I opened up my 16 in single shot spurts and one went down. King had circled around and now attacked the sword arm of the second man and rounded up wrestling him to the ground. The man yelling and screaming like I only wish I could. The other man stopped dead in his tracks, when he saw King, and tried to get back to the others. Now he was the one with the "Bad idea"! A single burst, on "full-auto," and he went down in a heap.

The rest of the team was just finishing up the other five, as I got to them. In all the confusion, three of them did their own version, without the "yell," of course, and settled the score.

I knelt down to the team leader and he said, "good job!"

He asked, "But, where the hell did you get a yell, like that?"

I said, "John Wayne." We both had to laugh.

King came prancing up to us, wagging his tail, and I patted him and brushed him up with my fingers.

"Good boy, buddy!"

"You're the best, King!" The leader said.

"He saved our ass, today!"

The other four guys went over to assist the two wounded guys I was with and we all organized a secured "L-Z" for the next "taxi" to pick us up. It was already dark and the rain had started to come down. But, we weren't finished, yet.

It turned out, nobody escaped without something to remember this trip by. One man was gone, and we lost one "chopper." Four of us were hit and wounded, including the team leader and I, as it turned out got hit, I supposed, with a piece of the exploding helicopter, when it crashed. I never felt a thing until a few hours later and blood was noticed coming from behind my vest. I persuaded the others to get in close together, within a ten foot circle and that I'll have King on the outside, forming a sentry pick. Nobody said a word and they had the fullest confidence in my big guy.

112

Word had been sent back telling of our situation but they couldn't send anybody out in this kind of wind and rain. It would've been just no good. So we had to wait it out. A couple of guys went to sleep, knowing King would get them up if something went down, but the team leader crept up to me to keep me company. Because of King I placed myself a little outside the circle and towards the trail. I figured if anything was to go down, it was to be from there it would come. He asked if I had any "butts," but I told him "I don't smoke." I offered him a stick of gum, instead, and he said, "Thanks."

"By the way, my name is Diaz, Sgt. Emilio Diaz. What's yours?"

I told him John, and that I was from the "City."

"Yeah? Me too!" "The Bronx, Man, Boogie-Down!"

"Just my luck," I kidded, "to be stuck here with a Yankee Fan!"

"Oh man, you're not with the Mets, are you?"

"Yeah! I was a Brooklyn Dodger, until they left for La-La." " Yeah, that was the "joint," back in doze days." "Hey, you did good, today. You represent Brooklyn, alright, you know?"

"Thanks. Taking out that supply ditch was cool, too!"

"Hey, yeah, how about that shit, not giving me the ok, to blow that thing? What the hell is going on around here, lately? A lot of double-talking "chicken shit", if you ask me." It's just one extraction after another. Like they won't even let us fight, anymore. You know, more guys get messed up on extractions than on the actual patrol. That's probably when our weakest point is and the best time for "Charlie" to hit us. Look at what happened, today!" I nodded my head to him remembering what Pete had told us.

"Yeah, It's becoming a shame, man. I hear that Nixon is trying to get some kind of talks underway, to close this show down."

I say. "Well, something has got to happen and soon. We just can't be doing this, forever, like in Korea. How bad is that? Nobody wants to finish, anymore." "I tell him, I hear all this crap about how we're losing this thing and everyone is doing drugs and this and that. And, I say, I can't believe people, back home is believing this stuff."

He says, "People want to believe because they're afraid, man. They want some justification to protest and not go. They'll grab on to anything, even this bullshit, to justify them not being called. And, most guys blaming their problems with drugs on this duty, man, had that problem, long before they came here. You tell me," he says, "Would you let your dog goof off on you? No! And, would I allow you to front me and my men if you came into this messed up? Hell No! So why do these people think we're always on drugs or something? I tell you, man, somebody got to be raking in the dough on this one, for it to last so long. What a crock! I just hope, one day, I can see the truth comes out."

After a while I asked Diaz what he would expect in the coming hours.

"Well, I can't see them sending out another chopper until at least the morning. "Charlie knows we're here but doesn't know much else. So I expect them to be crawling around, out there, trying to get a read on us and also trying to salvage whatever is left from that cache. But, I wouldn't expect much until morning."

I'm exhausted but I won't go to sleep on King. I've never done that and he's never done it with me. Sort of like a little silent clause in our "partnership" agreement.

Diaz checks his men and I get up slowly to not disturb anybody and to stretch my legs. The rain is letting up a little and the wound in my chest has stop bleeding with the patch one of the guys put on me a few hours ago. I know the word has gotten back and I wonder what the reaction was to it. "Probably, just another casualty on the scoreboard." Just another number added to the list on the TV screen, back home.

"Yo, man. Gotta stop this shit!" I determine. "It's not good to be thinking like this."

It gets to be about 5:40M.M. Light now starts to appear in the eastern sky. I wonder what it'll bring.

I've long ago stopped trying to compete with King as far as detecting any alerts. It's almost embarrassing comparing King's natural abilities when it comes to mine. In most cases it's my imagination that "sees" something, only to find out later it was a tree or bush. But with experience my "sight vision" is now unimpeded. I only have to look five feet to see what my "buddy" is doing. I just wonder, sometimes, if he ever has an imagination, too. And, what he either "knows" or "thinks" about. I study this dog and I'm convinced they know more than they give out. Just like that dog, in the demo show, getting up and "peeing" on that handler's leg. That still brings me a smile of a day from what seems another lifetime ago.

Daylight starts to take effect so I start stirring up the guys, praying the rest did some good for yesterday's wounds. Everyone is still accounted for, thank God, and we try to dig in a little more for whatever is coming our way, and, for who gets here first. Much to my surprise one of the guys had his radio on all night long and he says, "Baseball season starts today!"

He pumps his fist and gives out with a "Yo, Dodgers!"

I look at Diaz incredibly.

"You let this Los Angeles team-stealer on your mission?"

Diaz smiles and says, "He didn't take my team!"

We both smile as our predicament is momentarily, "miles away."

"Hey! How about those Jets! Let's go Mets!" I respond. That makes everybody groan, just a little bit, except King.

He's been the only one paying attention to the developing situation as we try to forget. He gives me an unmistakable alert in the direction of the jungle off to our left as he jumps up and growls staring in that direction. That stirs us back to reality.

"OK, be alert, you guys, we have company," says Diaz.

One guy whispers, hopefully.

"Could it be the chopper?"

"No," Diaz says, "The chopper would be coming in from the direction, the dog is looking in now".

Sure enough, King is up and fidgety. He's looking in two different directions. The problem is who's going to get here first. And we don't want what happened yesterday, to happen, again.

I get up and look at Diaz. He knows what I'm thinking. He's a good man. We got to bring the fight to "Charlie" to buy some time for the Huey to land and get the wounded on board. Then, hopefully, get back for us. Remembering Pete and Ranger, I say it straight to Diaz.

"I just want one promise from you, Yankee."

"Yeah?"

"If anything happens to me and King is in good shape, you take him back, with you. Don't you don't leave him behind, no matter what anyone says. I don't care if Westmoreland is on the chopper. You understand?"

"I got it? But in case you never heard, before, no one ever gets left behind, on the field of battle, with Rangers. We have that tradition. OK now, let's get over to that wreck and see what we got."

"Thanks, Diaz, besides, King here comes from the "CITY," too!"

"You're kidding!" Ha! " The three of us from the Apple? Does Charlie's know this?"

As we set up next to the downed chopper, we check out our equipment and ourselves. Diaz says, "Hey! We get out of this how about a couple of hot dogs and a beer, at Nathan's, man?"

"With a Yankee fan? I got the first round. King, too!" Diaz says.

"Yeah," I say, as I look down at the big guy. He looks up at me as I pat and rub his head.

"Yeah, buddy, you especially!"

The sound of the chopper becomes more apparent as it approaches the L-Z. Still no sign of "Charlie," We know they're out there waiting.

As the chopper hovers and lands, we start shooting up the jungle and throw grenades in the direction King was looking in. Still no return fire and we really don't know how effective we are. They load up the wounded men quickly and signal for us to get over there. We're about 100 feet away.

Diaz signals for King and I to go. He'll cover.

I get to the Huey and load King on board and then turn around to cover for Diaz, as he makes his break.

It is only now that I realize the dust being kicked up in the dirt around Diaz as he runs for the chopper. I also hear those "mosquitoes", again, pinging off the chopper. I still keep firing my m-16 and am joined by the 50. Caliber machine gun, on the gunship. Half the jungle seems to be falling down in the barrage. Diaz gets to the chopper and in all one-motion jumps in without any assistance. King is barking for me to get on and as we take off the 50cal. is still blowing up the trees and surrounding landscape. The crew chief from the chopper asks if everyone is "ok"?

"Yeah, we'll be fine. Thanks, man!"

"That's our job!" he says.

"Some job!" I say. "I wouldn't want it."

"Me too!" says Diaz.

The chief laughs, "Well, that's good because I wouldn't do what you guys do, either. I hate Snakes!"

We all unwind a bit.

All of a sudden, "Dodger fan says, "Man, They shot Jim Morrison!"

"What?"

"I was listening to the Doors, man, on the radio. His new song, "Touch Me", and then he shows us his new radio his folks just sent him for Christmas. It has a bullet hole in it. Right through the speaker!

Diaz, trying to relax, now, closes his eyes and pulls his hat over his face.

"I bet you they wouldn't have shot Santana", he smirks.

Chapter XXI
A BAD SITUATION

I was glad to get back to Tan Son Nhut and try to resume some semblance of normality.

As I walked off the plane with King, I was met at the landing pit with an ambulance and Susan, the attending nurse.

"You always meet the planes when they come in?"

"Shut-up and get in. Open your mouth," she ordered as she stuck a thermometer in my mouth. She then grabbed my wrist and looked at her watch for about thirty seconds. After she was finished she took the thermometer out of my mouth and, then looked around the fast moving truck speeding over the tarmac, with the siren blaring towards the infirmary, to see if anybody was watching. The other guys disembarked at Pleiku and Diaz and me promised each other those hotdogs and beers at Nathan's, one day, soon. Seeing the opportunity, Susan then kissed me a most beautiful welcoming kiss I've had in a very long time.

Breathlessly, I try to get my composure back.

"You're going to have to stop meeting all these planes that land here. I wouldn't like it and you won't have any more lips, by the time you go home."

"How dare you get yourself all screwed up like that. And, I thought your dog was going to protect you?"

I try to half-heartedly hold her off me.

"Hey! Don't even go there. I wouldn't be here, now, if it weren't for him."

I bent over and patted my tired and muzzled partner.

"Although he's not doing a great job of it now!"

He just keeps looking at the nurse, but not once does he do anything threatening towards her.

"I'm sorry. It was just that we kept an open transmission on you and me and your friend Luker listened to everything that was happening. I was going crazy. Luker kept measuring me that King was 'the best' and he wouldn't let anything happen to you." I kissed her again, just as we were backing up the ambulance to the infirmary.

The doors swung open and Luker and a few of the guys were there to meet us. King and I jumped out but Susan stayed on.

"Is he fit for duty, Lieutenant?" someone asked, and she said, "Yes, he's fit and very capable to carry out his duty", smiling.

A few smirks and then Luker says, "I got the first round!"

"Would you like to accompany us, sir?"

"No, thanks. Not this time. But, I know where you are!

I just smiled and acknowledged my 'thank you', to her. She smiled back.

On the way, I drop off King and shower at the kennels. I then changed my clothes with the ones Luker had so thoughtfully brought along. It was good to be back home.

The six-pack dropped the six of us at the airman's club, but the sarge mentioned not to get "stupid."

"Some of you guys are working, tonight."

It was close to six o'clock when it was just Luker and I. The others had left to report for work and it was already dark with the usual rain was coming down. We were off for the night because of our recent "moon-lighting" up-country. It wasn't because we were overflowing with handlers.

We have already lost the guys from the 1st. detachment of handlers, who rotated back to the world," and taking away the casualties, we were about 50% undermanned. A plan to recruit volunteers only produced a few not nearly enough takers and they were still in training with their new dogs. The last option was to start training the Vietnamese how to work with the dogs. We all could see where that was going to lead and we didn't much care for it at all. On a much brighter hope, we were expecting a new contingent of handlers to come in from the states any day-now, but, as yet, they still hadn't arrived.

"So what's the story?" I asked.

"Well it's not good. There's a lot of talk about transferring OJT guys into K-9 from other outfits. They are mostly guys who don't want to be here in the first place. Then there's the stuff of giving the dog's over to the ARVN's. Whatever it is, there aren't any more dogs coming in. The scaling back has already started. These are the last dogs to come over and that's why no dogs are going to be allowed to leave. That crap about the dog's being sick was just trumped up. It turned out to be a tick from Malaysia that some of the British dogs carried in with them. But, none of the dogs that didn't come in any contact with those dogs ever developed anything. The Vet has this medicine, Tetracycline that straightens it right up.

How's King? He's fine, isn't he? So is 'Blo. I don't see any of the stuff they're saying. To me, it's a cop-out. They're 'tap-dancing', man, big time."

"I know! They're saying too many stories." I say. "Now, it's because the dogs would be too dangerous to be around other people. I really think these dogs are smart enough to handle the situation. They know who the bad guys are. You know, I was on that ambulance, today, with Susan, and nothing happened, with king. NOTHING! When we're on the choppers with the other guys, nothing happens. Right? I say these dogs are a lot smarter than everybody gives them credit for. Sometimes King seems to read my mind, man. And, in a lot of cases, he's way ahead of me! He can tell when to goof off or when it's serious time or even when to "disappear" and not bother me, because of a mood I'm in. People, don't even do that! Flat-out, we wouldn't have made it this far without them. We all know that. We've got to get them out of here, Luke. HELL! We're the ones who brought them here!"

Susan, in civilian clothes, wearing a white blouse, short sleeve, and black dress pants, looking real sharp, walks up to the table.

"We owe it them, Luke!"

"And, we owe what to whom?"

We both get up from the table.

"I apologize, err, Susan?"

"Yes, and if I hear a 'sir' or a 'Lieutenant,' tonight, I'll shoot you."

I ask, "But, err, this is an 'enlisted' man's club. How, why?"

"Because I knew you guys would be here and I'm your 'guest', for the evening. Besides, my 'date' with the General fell through. Now, what's good here to eat and, speaking of owing, what does a lady have to do to get a drink around here"

"And, I'm sorry Luke, Vanessa had to work tonight. She would definitely like another chance with a rain-check, however."

"You tell her she's got it." In the meantime, lady and gentleman, please excuse me. I've got some boots to shine." "See you later, brother!"

"By the way, don't forget about that 'demo' tomorrow, at the kennels."

"What demo?" Susan asks.

"We're bringing in some ARVN's, to allow them to see the dogs for becoming possible replacement handlers." I respond.

"You got to kidding me," she laughs. "Who came up with that idea?"

Seeing how disgusted I am, she stops laughing.

"Can I go? I would just love to see the dogs."

"You wanna be a replacement, too?"

"Maybe," she answers, with a lovely cuteness, I could never say 'no' to. But, I smile.

"Why not, what dog could resist your charms?"

"None, around here, I hope!"

After a while and an appetizer, she a wine spritzer and I have a scotch sour she asks, "What's going on with you two?"

"Nothing, you look beautiful, tonight." She really did! It was actually the first time I saw her in a "normal setting," with real clothes and although she wasn't the kind for too much make-up, she did have a touch on, now. Her brown hair was now out of her "working mode" and its silky shiny texture accented her shoulders and the shape of her back perfectly. The glow from the table candle allowed her blue eyes to twinkle like a star.

We talked all through dinner about ourselves and how we got here and at about 10:30 p.m. she mentioned she was going to have to leave.

"The morning comes very quickly and the work never stops." I could see she likes what she is doing and knows she is doing what she can, in this war.

"Just a few minutes more," I asked.

"John, what's the matter? You have a lot on your mind."

"The doctor, Captain Mallory, is he still here?"

"Yes, but, I think he will be leaving, soon, to go back home."

"God Bless!" I say.

"I'd like to talk with him for a few minutes. Could you arrange it?"

"Yes, of course, but is it an emergency?"

"No, and then, yes. It can be, really! I'd just like a consult."

"Ok, how about the day after tomorrow?"

"Fine, that would be great!"

"John, really, is there something wrong?" As we get up and head for the door, I grab her hand and place it on my chest, next to an open button.

"OH, yeah, nurse! Right there! I need something real bad for the pain."

As we leave the warmth and comfort of the airmen's club and step out into the rain and darkness, we walk in the direction of her nursing hootch. Her hand now reaches inside my half open shirt and we kiss a very deep kiss.

"Is this where it hurts?"

Unfastening another button her hand moves, "Does it hurt here?" I bring her closer to me as I can feel her mouth gently kissing the spot. Licking the raindrops off my chest, we close our eyes momentarily to the world and it's problems.

The next day was dark and eerily overcast and breezy. Heavy clouds threatened to burst open at any minute as if it was an omen. It was, now, we saw a glimpse of the future. And no one liked what they saw.

A detachment of about nine ARVN (South Vietnamese) soldiers pull up to the kennels and at the ordering by this little guy in a captain's uniform, they start unloading their equipment. They were the "volunteers" that came to learn how to work the dogs.

At first none of them wanted to get off the truck. Then, no one wanted to be the first to see any of the dogs, up front and personal. I had to smile and I immediately remembered my first day with King and said, to myself, "NO WAY" was this going to happen."

The Sgt. asked the little guy, in charge, "Who volunteered, these guys?"

The ARVN Captain replied, "Oh, they all are very serious."

At that moment, Luker walks out of the hootch with Diablo and all the ARVN run back on to the truck. The Captain starts to yell and scream at his men in Vietnamese and we all knew what was going to happen then. All the dogs in the back started going crazy and barking. The louder the Captain chastised and cajoled his men to get off the truck the louder the dogs got in the back of the hootch. Not to mention Diablo. Although muzzled and held tightly by Luke, it was all he could do to hold him. Somehow, the ARVN Captain started to notice that ol' Diablo was looking at him and he began to tone down his antics to his men. The soldiers didn't want any part of this and we were glad to agree with them.

The captain boarded back on the truck and left. I had a vision that if this were a cartoon or something all the dogs would have been chasing them down the road, yelling and screaming. But, I only reasoned it was all just a matter of time. "They'll be back."

Susan who was up at the kennels expecting to see a demo, staged for the ARVN's was "disappointed". She settled for a personal tour of the kennels and a meeting with King. She, of course, was on the outside of the fenced off exercise area, but, after a brief work-through, I walked King over to her. She knelt down and very deliberately, but softly said hello to King. It was the very first time I saw a sweetness of the big guy to another person, whom he didn't know. With true gentleness he put his nose up against the fence and allowed Susan to touch him through the fence. Not at all did I feel any threatening gestures or moves.

"I thought you said he was a killer? Sorry, this must be the wrong dog." King and I looked at each other. He wasn't the "wrong" dog.

I brought King back to his area and patted him down and met Susan outside the hootch.

"I have three dogs back home, in Ohio, that are very close to me."

"I can see you get along pretty well with them."

"Yes, I'm very fortunate. I love them too. But now, I'm going to have to get ready for work."

"Can I take you back to the infirmary?"

"OK," she says, "By the way how's your pain, this morning"

"A whole lot better, but I might need someone to follow up on the therapy."

"Oh, that's too bad! There's only one way to get that medicine and it's in very short supply. I'll also be seeing the Captain so I'll set up your meeting with him."

"Great, I would really be appreciative."

"And, you're still not going to tell me what's it all about?"

"Susan, better off left unsaid, for now. Besides, it may never happen, so what's to say?"

"OK, call me in the morning and I'll tell you the best time to come over to the infirmary."

"Good, it'll give me an excuse to see you again."

"You don't need an excuse," she says, as she gets out of the six-pack, in front of the hospital tent.

"She's kind of special, ain't she?" says Luker from the back compartment of the moving truck, now lifting up the canvas covering, as we head to our hootch.

"Yeah! And where the hell did you come from…."

"Man, you got more stuff up inside your eyes, lately over that girl, if I was king I'd sue for divorce. You had best get your mind back on the ground, bro!"

Luker and I were patrolling connecting sentry posts, that evening and that gave us all night to get our plan together. After our initial sweep of the area we meet up at the intersection of the posts.

"Ok, I'm going to talk with that doctor Captain, tomorrow. I'm going to trust him with what we want to do."

"Dee, listen, we really can't do this. As much as we feel, man, they're still government property."

"Yeah, and they're just going to give them to what? What we saw, today? No, way, man! They don't even want the dogs! You saw it. They hate the dogs from their own superstitions and religious beliefs. The VC wants them dead so bad they put a goddamn bounty on us. Do you think they're gonna treat them the way they should? Hell, they won't even feed them properly."

"Yeah, I know. The dogs eat better than they do now", adds Luker.

"Luke, they have no use for these dogs and our government don't want to bring them back. We ain't even allowed to win this goddamn thing and all they want to do is to get out. Do you think the hats in Washington are going to worry about a few dogs? Hell, I feel we're lucky that they even considering bringing us back."

"Luke, not for nothing, but we've been left here by our own government, man. They want to close this show down and forget it ever happened. You can hear it in their words and deeds, man. And, forget about the people. They were the first one's to jump ship."

Luker was just silent but I could tell he was thinking hard.

"Luke, if no one cares, then we got to care about them and ourselves. I'm not going anywhere without him." I felt King's nose on my hand and I began rubbing his head.

"I know he wouldn't leave me."

"OK," What's the plan?"

"Let's make another sweep and meet back here in about an hour." Smiling, I said, "We should have one by then." Ha!

Luke shrugged his shoulders, "Oh, shit! It's gonna be like that, again, eh? By the skin of our ass!"

"They're the best kind!"

All through the night and a steady drizzle but thankfully, no rain, we plotted and schemed but nothing of any practical reality came to us.

"Don't worry, it'll come. We've got time, still", I said, out loud. But, I murmured, to myself, "God, please, let it be." I knew Luke was ok, because he now sounded like me.

"You know, I wasn't going to leave him, here. I don't think any handler feels any different than us but we all have different methods."

I tell him, "I want you to come with me, tomorrow, to see the doctor. He may have a prescription for what ails us."

Susan told me to come over about 11:30A.M. Luke and I arrive promptly for our appointment, in front of the infirmary. The sky is still overcast as it's been since "forever" it feels, but not raining. We walk in and ask the nurse to see Doctor Mallory.

"He's in the ward. I'll buzz him to let him know you're here."

"Thank you!"

Vanessa comes out first to say "hello." She's beautiful. A statuesque girl, about 5''11" and makes her fatigue scrubs look good.

In an angelic whisper of a voice, "Hi, John. I'm Vanessa, Susan's friend."

"She's from Gary, Indiana." adds a goofy, smiling Luker.

"I was with Wayne and Susan, listening to the radio transmissions of your patrol the other day. That was frightening. Is everything all right now? How are those other men?"

"Oh, yes, they're good! They're up in Pleiku."

"I have some friends up there. They'll be in good hands."

"I bet they are", Luker smirks, as I see him pretending to be sick and needing attention, in the background.

"And, you and your dog? You're doing better?"

"Susan is a good nurse. She really takes care of her patients well. Is she here, now?"

"Yes, she's inside but she's doing her rounds. She'll be out in a second."

I smile and nod, "Thanks", but I can't look at Luke. He is like a glass of water with a tiny little hole on the bottom. I can see this grown man's knee shake around this beautiful girl. And, he can't stand still. I have to turn my head for fear of laughing out loud, at this spectacle. I move over to a magazine rack and let them talk but seconds later the doctor comes out and welcomes the both of us.

"Come into my office."

"Thank you, sir!" I look at Luke and he lets go of Vanessa's hand, begrudgingly.

"I'll call you later, ok?"

"Vanessa smiles and acknowledges, "OK."

"And, I'm the one to get my feet back on the ground? And, I can't handle a woman", I admonish Luke walking through the big double doors, leading to the doctors private cubicle.

"Now, wait a minute. I can explain….", trying to tap-dance his way out of this.

We go into the next room, past some stretchers and a couple of empty beds and enter a tiny room with some graphs and charts on the make-shift board that cover some canvas partition.

"Tell it to me later, 'Doctor Love', we ain't got no time, now."

Still smiling at Luker, I address the "real" doctor, "Thank you, sir, for seeing us so soon. I'd like some information if I may ask."

"You want to know if I can help you get your dog out of country." My mouth drops open. The captain smiles, "You're about the tenth K-9 guy to ask me that question, in the last few weeks." Luker and I smile. "Good! I was beginning to wonder but I guess we all feel just about the same way."

"I'll tell you what I told them. I can't do too much from this side unless it's a "bang-bang" thing, too quick for anyone to notice, and not until it was too late for anyone to stop it. Do you have a plan or an idea?"

"We're working on it, but it is good to know you're with us, on this."

"Listen, I love dogs, too. I'm not saying I can do anything. I'm leaving in two months and after that you're going to have to begin again with whoever takes my place. And he may not feel the same way."

"We understand. Two months, that's not good! Doesn't give us much time. Damn! Excuse me, sir. It's not that we don't appreciate...."

"Don't worry about that, you've got to get something in place. And, soon!"

My head was full with thought as we left the infirmary. So much as to almost forget to see Susan. She had to run out the front doors to stop us from leaving, altogether.

"Hey, weren't you guys going to say hello?"

"Oh, God. I'm sorry. Of course we were. I was just thinking."

"You sure were! And, so was I. Are we still going to have lunch?"

"Yes! Yes, that's a good idea."

The three of us head over to the Exchange, where they have a little lunch counter/table set-up place and a jukebox. We all order a hamburger and fries with a coke and sit at one of the tables, near the window.

"They better have some Mo-Town in this box" Luke says, as he approaches the machine to play some records.

As the coins drop in the slot, I hear him sing, "Stand by Your Man", sing it, Tammy!"

I smile and look at Susan.

"He's a goof", she says.

"And, he sure knows his way around women", I smirk. He's real smooth with your girlfriend, Vanessa.

"She's beautiful, isn't she?" Susan remarks.

"She sure is, honey", Luker says sitting back down at the table, recapturing his "smoothness".

"Cuter than Diablo?" She asks.

"Now, lady, you should know by now, never to go there. Totally, two different strokes of paint for the house."

"Never quite heard it said like that, before", I add, smiling.

Smokey and the Miracles start singing on the jukebox.

"Beautiful song, right there, partner", he says.

"Listen to those words. Pure poetry, my man", he says.

"Sing it Smokey!"

Our burgers arrive at the table and we begin to eat, but I'm not really that hungry.

Susan catches me looking out the window at the distant mountain range and my thoughts drifting and lost.

Trying to bring me back to the table, she asks about my little conversation with Diaz and his men about the different types of music we were talking about and liking.

I smile again and I just explain how I've found how important music can be to one's perception and attitude. How it forms an aura or how it can accent an opinion.

"Take the big band sound, of the forties. It gave us an enthusiasm and united fortification. It encouraged teamwork against a common foe that got us through the war. I may be wrong, but they'll never capture another moment like that, again."

Oh, Com'mon, Luker chimes in, "Today's music has got to be the best! Look at all the different variations. From county-Western to Opera, there is something for everyone to sink their teeth into."

"I love the Beatles." Says Susan.

"No, I agree", I admit. "But, today's music seems to always have an edge or a message for people to interpret. What about just for the sake of enjoyment and entertainment? Why can't it be fun, again?

"Well, it seems to me that if you enjoy it, it would be fun." Luke motions, as he starts to move his body in sync to the music." It's all in the rhythm, partner, ha! And, listen to those words!"

Susan now gets up to dance with Luker.

"Are you sure this is how the cavemen did it", Susan asks Luker.

"I swear, it's the truth!" The records now change in the jukebox.

I'm smiling at these two, when the next song comes on. It's a more somber song and the mood shifts.

"See that's what I mean." I continue. "The music can dictate a tempo or mood. It can also magnify it! When you're watching a movie, for instance, you don't even notice the background music accompanying the scene, but it all produces the desired effect. It helps define the moment."

We all agree, "We got to have the music! Ha!"

We're having fun, but a void has been created by our individual thoughts of facing our present situation. Only the music is heard, for a long time when Susan finally breaks the spell.

"You know you can't do it, right?" she finally says. My attention comes immediately back to the table and I look directly into her eyes.

"We have to try!"

"Oh, OH!" I hear Luker say.

"What?" I say"

"John, I wasn't eavesdropping. I was in the next cubicle, around the canvas partition, taking care of my patient. I swear! But, yes, I heard the whole thing between you and the doctor. You just can't do that! What will happen if you get caught?"

"I don't know and I don't care, Susan. This whole thing is a sham! There are a whole lot of dog-loving people out there. Maybe, if we can ever get that far and the word get out, along with everything else this stinking mess represents. Maybe nothing. Maybe everything. But, we just may be able to get our 'souls' back. We just can't leave these dogs here. Jesus, girl, they'll wind up being killed and eaten, ferchristsakes! You see what these people eat. These dogs would be a staple!"

Luke now chimes in, "They sure ain't going to use them for any fighting. The dogs are too big and uncontrollable. And, with all their beliefs about reincarnation and stuff, they would believe they would turn into a dog, in their next life, if they were ever killed with one."

"Susan, the whole thing is wrong! Ever hear of Destiny? We may be here for only one thing; to prevent this tragedy."

Silence, again, comes over the table as the next record begins to play. Marvin Gaye and Tammy Terrell, "Ain't No Mountain High Enough."

I look down at the table and smile.

"Good song, partner! And, how true! See what I mean about music?"

We head back to the infirmary and nobody is saying anything. It's dusty on the road as the wind is blowing in from the sea. The sky, as always, is overcast. We just kind of left it that we'll get in touch, but, I felt a little strange, as she entered the doors of the hospital. I looked at Luke, but he just shrugged his shoulders. We hurried back to our hootch as the wind really started to kick up and tried to relax a little. But, I kept on thinking about "only two months left" the doctor had said. It just wasn't enough time.

As the time approached to get ready for work, I hear the Mets had won again on the radio and that they were causing some excitement in the baseball pennant race back home. Sure, who would figure? Being a Mets fan ever since they came into existence, in 62', and rooting for them even though they were the "clowns princes of baseball", it would have to happen while I am halfway around the world and man is planning to land on the moon, they become good. There is no doubt about the irony to me, if that it could happen. Regardless of all the chaos and confusion in the world, these historic moments were occurring, too.

"Maybe there is room for just one more miracle, yet!"

Chapter XXII
TRANSFER TO THAILAND

When we arrived at the kennels, on the deuce 12, the sarge tells me to go in and see the Captain. I knocked on the door and entered the hootch. Dwight Knowles was already there and they were waiting for me.

"Hello, John, I want you and Ike to pack your bags, you're leaving."

"SIR?" I looked, at Ike and it seems he has been already told.

"You two are going to one of our bases in Thailand and it may be you won't be back, again."

Ike asks if he knew which one, and the Captain says, "Probably our B-52 base at Utapoa, in the south." Pointing to the map on the wall. You've been there before and know the terrain.

"As you are aware, we've other bases in Thailand that support all air traffic here. As part of a review, I'm required; so let me quickly go over this with you, again, briefly."

"In the North, on the Laotian border, fighting the Pathet Lao, the Laotian communists, is Non Kom Phenom, "NKP". Towards the central part are our F-85's and other combat fighters at Ubon, Tahkli and Udorn. Your base carries the big boys, the B-52's and KC-135, fuel tankers carrying that fuel for the fighters and our other strategic air missions.

All reports from intelligence indicate "Charlie" wants to broaden the war and drag in these other three countries; Cambodia, where all their sanctuaries lie; Laos, supplied by the Communists and Thailand, an ally of ours since World War II. You know they would love to get a crack at the B-52's, while they're laying on the ground, since they can't hit them in the air."

I was kind of struck "speechless," needless to say, until finally I ask, "When is the move?"

"Tomorrow, you're not working, tonight. Go back and pack and be back here in the morning at 7:00 A.M. The six-pack will pick you up with your equipment at the hootches at 6:40 A.M. Any other questions?"

"No, Sir" "Gentlemen, Good Luck and God Speed." shaking our hands.

As we leave the office, I ask Ike, "What happened?"

He responds, "I don't know. When they called me, I thought they were going to transfer me out to security, because of me losing my dog."

"But, that wasn't your fault. That could've happened to anyone."

"Dee, I carry a deep guilt for that dog, dammit!" He said as tears well up in his eyes.

Dwight, known as "Ike," was on a recon patrol outside of DaNang, up north, with a marine detachment, when his dog pushed him out of the way and took the full brunt bite of one of the thousands of poisonous snakes that inhabit the region. The region is also the home of the "King Cobra," possibly the most dangerous snake in the world.

It is said and studied that it was the "cobra" that is so prominently mentioned throughout the Bible, representing the Devil. It will slither and move so silently that it can encircle you without you knowing it and then use it's body and weight, which can grow up to 45 feet, in length, to then hold you in place as it slowly crushes you to death. This is what happened to Ike's dog. And, even though the snake was killed by the feverous efforts of the patrol, the muscle reflex continued by the snake until the dog had to be killed just to put it out of its misery.

"But instead, they told me about the move and that I'll be getting Pete's old dog, Ranger."

I told Ike I'd be with him in a few minutes for the ride back to the living hootch, "I just want to see King for a second and to tell Luker what happened."

I go to the back of the kennels and see Luke muzzling up Diablo. I go over to pat down King. He's wagging his tail at my approach, as always, waits for us to get to work. It always perks up my spirit to receive his welcoming. I tell Luker and he's in shock. But, then to my surprise he starts to smile.

"No wait, this might be what the "doctor ordered.""

"What?"

"Don't you see, man. You're out of here and much closer to Sak, who've I've always maintain was going to be the one true help, in this plan, anyway."

I was trying to see what Luke was talking about, when I hear Ike calling me to get on the leaving six-pack.

"Talk to me in the morning." I yell to Luke as we leave for the return trip.

When we arrive back at the hooch I begin to gather all my stuff and start loading up my duffle bag. I really can't believe I'm actually leaving this hell and going back to Thailand. This whole thing just happened too fast, but soon mixed emotions started a war inside me.

I won just by surviving and I'm bringing King out of it, too! But, I'm leaving some beautiful men behind and that doesn't sit too well with me, either. And, what about Susan? I've got to tell her! Looking at my watch, which says 8:30P.M, now, I immediately try calling her at her quarters but I'm told she isn't there. I ask for her to call me as soon as she gets in and then return to my packing.

Unbelievable, all the little things that seem important at isolated moments in the course of living that people keep. I planned to keep everything that I ever came in touch with me for the last nine months, as reminders, but I was rapidly running out of space in my bag.

I had apparently lied down for a moment's rest, for when I finally awoke the ceiling light was shining in my eyes and my neck hurt from the contortion I found myself in. I felt like I must have been on a three-day drunk and I immediately questioned whether or not I had imagined my reassignment. That however was quickly dispelled as I trip over my three quarter filled duffle bag, that I left in the middle of the floor of the hooch. It was now 3:45A.M. I had not had a return call from Susan. I felt an empty feeling in my stomach but what could I do? We just felt very differently about something extremely important to me, My Best friend, King. And, as strange as that may be for anyone to understand, to me it was really quite simple. No other alternative was comprehensible. I did feel bad, however, for now time had run out for us. I would always feel that if we had some more we could have resolved some of our differences of opinion.

I felt a little better as I took a shower and just let the water run over my body. By the time the handlers come in from their night patrols, I was ready and we loaded up the waiting six-pack. We stopped off for a cup of coffee at the mess hall for breakfast.

I was always struck funny to see the reaction of the other personnel in the mess, when they would catch a glimpse of us having breakfast. They would be all polished and shiny new in their fresh and laundered uniforms, having had a full night's sleep and just starting out the new day fresh and as clean as a daisy.

K-9, in comparison, looked like "twenty miles of very bad road." Filthy and muddy from frolicking in the monsoon driven quagmire of jungle and swamps, these other men probably never knew existed.

Sweaty and smelly and mostly unshaven, it was these unheralded men and their loyal, devoted partners who made sure "Charlie" wasn't going to interrupt their sleep. Yet, they all made elaborate and most exaggerated paths to avoid any of us, at all costs, it seemed. Needless to say, we never had any problems getting a few tables together at the mess hall.

Sitting there now for the last time, a whole flood of memories came to me and filled my eyes.

"Do you remember the time that big sonafabitch, Van Ryan, came in for his favorite breakfast,"

"Scrambled eggs and bacon, right?" said Ike, "Yeah, and then he sat down at the table with those three guys who must've been from personnel, with those clean, tailored 1505's uniforms on."

"Oh Jesus," cried Luker, "They didn't know whether to shit or go blind. Remember that?" HA! HA! HA!

"They didn't talk. All they did was stuff they're mouths as quickly as possible, without swallowing, and tried to get out of there." Ike said, laughing.

"I thought that guy whose glasses kept falling off was going to start crying." I added, "The best part was when Van tried to start a conversation with them and asked them where they were from."

"Van was big bastard, though. What was he? SIX, SEVEN?"

"Yeah, easy, and in good shape, too." says, Luke. "And with all those weights, him and Cappy use to do. He was intimidating for anybody."

"Not for Clint Eastwood." I say smiling. "He'd kick his ass."

We all had a good laugh at where the absurdness of the conversation was going.

Leaving the mess Hall for the ride back to the kennels, now, was a time to face reality.

"They are going to break up a good team, man," said Luker. We grab each other's hand and hug each other.

"Remember, what I said and keep in touch."

"Yeah, let me see what the situation is over there and with any luck we'll coordinate a rendezvous in Bangkok," I say.

"Will be looking forward to it, buddy. You take care and let King get you home, man."

I wink. "We got to have you and Diablo over for dinner, soon!"

"OK, you guys. Let's get your dogs", yells the sgt., driving the six-pack.

We had past the infirmary on our way out to the kennels and I looked for Susan, but had no such luck. I feel bad about that but it was her decision and I wish her well. She is one of the many great people being swept up in this lousy situation. People should be held responsible for this terrible waste.

Chapter XXIII
UTAPOA, ROYAL THAI AIR FORCE BASE

"Over this war and all Asia is another reality: the deepening shadow of Communist China. The rulers in Hanoi are urged on by Peking.

"We are there because we have a promise to keep. Since 1954 every American President has offered support to the people of South Viet Nam."

Summary of Secretary of Defense Robert S. McNamara's Memo to President Lyndon B. Johnson:
July 20,1965

When we get to our destination the weather is overcast and very similarly dreary. I'm glad things haven't changed that much. Our C-130 lands just long enough to let us unload our equipment and get the crates, our dogs are in, off. Soon, the big plane is taxiing into position and then rumbles down the huge runway of Utapoa, Royal Thai Air Force Base.

This tremendous complex is still in the building stages at many points from when we were last here. The serene natural beauty of its landscape off the Gulf of Siam and a magnificent wonderland of vegetation and mountain ranges, which serves as a lovely backdrop to the Gulf water, can deceive any casual visitor of the dangers and horrors of man's creation just a few kilometers from here. It's almost unfathomable that man can find the time to wage war in this tropical paradise.

A muddy blue six-pack comes rumbling up to me and Ike and slams to a stop.

"Sorry to be late, I'm Sgt. Riechmuth. I'm with the K-9 detachment here at Utapoa. Welcome."

"Hello, Sgt., I'm John and this is Ike Knowles."

We had already let King and Ranger out of their uncomfortable and restrictive traveling crates and they were just noising around the immediate area, on short leash.

"Just as soon as they finish their water, we'll load up." I say.

"Great, good to have you guys, here. You're going to like this place. Specially, from the place you've just come from." Says Riechmuth. I reminding him that I was here, temping, some months ago but, Tan Son Nhut was our home and it had its good sides, too!"

The Sgt continues", I didn't know that but wait until you see this place, now, and our new kennel area. We have all new modern construction and it's thoughtfully laid out with an activity area that puts anyplace else to shame. They're putting tremendous money in this place as if we're going to be here a long time, unlike Nam, where everything seems so temporarily."

We nod and smile appreciatively, "That's encouraging," I say.

The Sgt. continues, "We're only about 80 miles from Bangkok," which raises my eyes, "and so far we're getting a night off every week and most of the guys use the break to go to this beach resort named Pataya. Not too far from here." "Now, that's how to fight a war!" Ike says, smiling.

Ike hadn't been with us when we were here for just a few days, the last time. This was all new to him. But, since we weren't allow to do much movement off base, the last, either, I had to definitely agree.

"This isn't so bad, King", rubbing his head. "What do you think, big fella? Not a bad little joint, right?"

Bad move on my part. No sooner than I said the magic word, "THINK" I immediately knew what was going to happen next. King looked directly at me and, as easy as can be, raises his hind leg up, as to relieve himself, at the idea of this place. Both, Ike, or Sgt, Riechmuth however never saw our little joke, before, and got hysterical. I guess it was probably *apropos*, after all.

Well, we all had a good laugh after I explained the story behind it. But, it dawned on me something much more profound. It's always been debated and argued whether animals can remember or otherwise reason or comprehend. I can say, without a doubt, they can. Dogs know a whole lot more than people understand, or "THINK."

We pack up the blue-colored truck and head around the bay area where the big B-52's are parked or being worked on and get waved through by the security sentry walking his post amongst all this activity and movement. He acknowledges us as we pass by and I wonder what he's thinking as he sees us with the big dogs.

"We're pretty much on our own, here, as not many know what to do with us." Says Riechmuth, "But we do all right with the limited force we have."

"How many dogs and handlers do we have, now?" I ask.

"With you and Ike we'll have sixteen teams, but we're getting a new detachment in by September that should double our size. Until then we can enlist volunteers but we don't have the dogs to fill out the slate. There was some talk of trying to get two maybe three guys with one dog, but that doesn't seem to be in the planning, anymore."

We pull around the perimeter road, which is actually off-base and we come to a stop next to a spanking brand new brick building and complex area with a loading dock and, I swear, "AIR CONDITIONING! I can't believe it!" I say, flabbergasted." Things have changed since I've been here."

Riechmuth laughs, "I told you, life is good!" "Wait till you see inside."

We quickly unload the truck and we let the dogs loose in the activity area, where the old headquarter hootch had been. There are all kinds of obstacles and other "play-things," there now, such as pads and ropes for the dogs to exercise their teeth, and to fool around with. Both, dogs seem comfortable in their new surroundings as they romp over some barriers and walls. As they amuse themselves, we get the tour of the compound.

I look at Ike and I'm encouraged to see an actual long-range plan in effect and being completed. Everything, brick and mortar and of sturdy "permanent" construction. It's nothing like the planks and wooden hootches that were around here, before. With the size of this installation and runway I could actually see a major international airport here, someday, serving this tropical wonderland with multitudes of tourists, and the capital, Bangkok, not very far away. If only people could get their act together.

Lt. Jamison comes out and greets us enthusiastically and introduces himself.

"Please come on in to my office. Would you care for any thing?

I say, "Thank you, sir, some water would be great!"

Knowles says the same and we settle in on some of the chairs in the office. From the window, I can see King walking around, sniffing out the terrain and starting to settle into his new home.

"Gentlemen, glad to have you here with us. I just want to give you the scoop on the story here I would rather you get it from me than somewhere else.

"Our mission here is basically containment and support. There have been a few small skirmishes, up north, around NKP on the Laotian border, but don't let that lull you about the potential of a major breakout here at any time. "Charlie" would love to get at these big birds, in the worst way. But, he's not the only game in town. Come over here and take a look at this map."

We get up and angle over to another desk in the corner of the office. There is a huge map, spread out, covering the whole Southeast Asian area. "We're here", as he points out a spot, south, on the map just on the tip of the Gulf of Thailand, formerly Siam. Moving north on the map he points out the other four air bases situated around the country, but, strategically near many of the potential hotspots, bordering some of the countries like Cambodia, Laos and in the far north, China. "Burma, over here on the left side, is pretty much, already under Communist control, although not much has been made of it and Malaysia just south, is constantly under siege. Now, let me tell you a little about this place, Thailand.

It has the longest running continuous form of government, the Monarchy, in the region. It's been in power for over five hundred years. Ever see the play, The King and I? We'll this was the place it depicted. However, Yul Brenner is not the King. Even during the Second World War, all the Japanese could do is sign treaties with this country. It was never fully under Japan's control, as were all the other countries, in this area, including Viet Nam, which is right here, as you well know, pointing to the other side of Cambodia, from Thailand.

Prince Sihanouk, of Cambodia, is out of control and losing land and power to the Khmer Rouge, or the Cambodian communists daily. He's in such a snit that he's been forced to ask Big Brother, up here, China, for assistance. China probably won't intervene, however, because the Cambodians trust them as much as the Vietnamese do. In this region, China has always been seen as "The Colossus of the North," and only the Japs are hated more. Another reason, they probably won't intervene is because of the close ties in this area to the Soviet Union, believe it or not, and the Russkies have ten motor divisions on their border with China, as we speak, just waiting for China to get distracted, here, for them to move in, there. So you see that's our only advantage, ancient animosities in the region and petty jealousies.

Everybody thinks it's China, but it's actually Mother Russia, we have to keep an eye on. Viet Nam gets all their oil and munitions from Russia. As we all know, the AK-47 rifle, the "VC" uses, is a Slavic weapon. Anything, however, could set off that powder keg between the big boys and then Viet Nam would only become an asterisk spot in history.

After our briefing, I say, "I thank you, sir, for your time in explaining all this to us. Has there been any hostile activity been taken against this facility, yet?"

"Extremely minor disturbances but there's been a marked increase up at NKP and our intelligence figures it's only a matter of time for them to get down here. You see the Cong don't get along too well, fortunately, with the Cambodian Communists. So it wouldn't be a walk in the park for them to cross Cambodia, at the present time, for them to hit us. But, if the Rouge, were to say, get "distracted", by the Chinese or by Sihanouk's loyalists, how long did it take for you to get here from Tan Son Nhut?"

Ike shakes his head in complete understanding and contemplation.

"So we just wait and see, right?"

"That's the story so far", says the Lieutenant.

"Oh. One more thing. We may be getting to experiment with a new weapon, designed just for K-9 and sentry night work. There's some talk of a telescope you can attach right onto your M-16's that uses new technology and illuminates star-light power and allows you to see in the dark."

"What? Is this for real?" I say, scratching my head.

"For real! We'll get to see it soon. But the one I'm opting for is the new modified M-15. This would be a single barrel sawed-off shotgun, holding six rounds in it's magazine. This could be strapped to your side and would take the place of the M-16 for us. This shotgun would eliminate the need for sighting and aiming in all practical situations, especially in the dark. Just pick a suspicious target and blow the sonafabitch away. That simple!"

"Pretty interesting stuff!" I say to Ike, as we bring our dogs in, to see their new home surroundings. Inside each individual cemented stall there is a big bucket of clean fresh water in an iron holder. They are easy to clean and sanitized. Best of all, there is a complete permanent roof to keep the dogs in out of the weather. A much preferred improvement than from which we had the last few months, for sure. I'm pleased and it shows through to King, I think he could get used to this.

After making sure everything was good, Ike and I jump back on the six-pack and Sgt. Reichmuth drives us over to our new living quarters. Instead of wooden and screened hootches, we now come up upon a "three story" barracks type cement complex. Just one in about a nine-structure "City." I couldn't believe it! "You've got to be kidding me!" I say.

Reichmuth laughs, "I told you, you will like this place."

"Does anybody else know about this?" Ike laughs. "Don't tell 'em."

Again, everything here seems to be on more of a "permanent basis." It's encouraging to say the least, and with the new contingent of American handler replacements, heading here, I feel a certain relaxation, for the first time in a long time. And, with Bangkok in close proximity, at the very least, I've gained the valuable time, now, to organize a workable plan and set into motion all the various intricate parts. I smile contently for the first time, too.

Even the weather appears to be brightening. The last couple of weeks of rain must wear on your nerves, somehow. Makes you "grumpy," You know?

Anyway we climb up to the second floor of our new "hotel" and Ike wonders why they didn't "put in an elevator?" We try to be as quiet as possible as most of the guys appear to be sleeping. One or two greet us and help us with our stuff and point out what's not being used. Like the kennels, half the barracks are ours for the taking and we decide to take the next to last one for ourselves, like we did for King and Ranger.

There are approximately five cubicles on each side of the gray painted corridor, down the middle of the floor space. Each of these cubicles can house four but it seems two, and in a few cases, three guys are the norm.

The only other activity are the house people, cleaning the muddy boots off last night's patrol and others just doing normal functions of cleaning. Ever since our episode with those agents for "Hanoi Hanna", I had lost a picture/photo album I had taken of my car, back home. It couldn't have meant much to anybody else, but to a eighteen year old, memories like that mean a lot. And, boy, time does move on! That reminds me to pick up some film for my camera. I must take some pictures of King, soon. He's growing up so fast.

I vow that although, I can't show King pictures of my car, I will have pictures, to show, of my best friend!

The next day we get to see what the perimeter territory looks like in the daylight. I appreciate that so I can make some mental notes about landmarks and points of interest to remember, when on patrol. It's important because everything takes on a different aspect and characteristic at night.

I like the prospect of getting those M-1 5 shotguns, because I always maintained how crazy it was to try and "aim" in the dark. In most cases, the men would just put the 16 on "fully auto" and spray the area. The shot gun with it's dispersal would be a much more effective weapon.

We're also shown how much area we should be covering but in actuality with only 16 dog teams what we can patrol. For the time being we're using the old tactic of "what ocean is the battleship is in", an old World War II tactic. Since we obviously don't have enough manpower to cover everything, we deploy randomly, show ourselves and let everybody know we're "here" and then secretly, a few hours later, regroup and then go to another area for redeployment. Everybody gets to know we're here and patrolling the sectors and the word gets around and everybody feels comfortable. Of, course, if something does happen in a sector and is detected by perimeter sentries, we have a quick response mobile unit, like K-SAT, to respond.

It's like putting up a sign warning of a vicious guard dog on your premises, but yet, not really having one. Let our "signs" advertise our K-9 patrols, but if we're "good," nobody should ever "see" us, until it's too late. "Charlie" is so spooked about K-9's ability, anyway, that they'll do anything to get away from us. Even raising the "bounty" on us. But, they don't want to take us on themselves. They're only friend was the surprise element, at night. Well. K-9 takes their "surprise" and gives them one back. The "night" is ours and the "VC" knows they lost it from the first moment K-9 step foot here. Before K-9 arrived "Charlie" could set up shop outside a facility and just bomb and mortar it at will. They would then slip back into the jungles when reaction teams would sweep the area in pursuit. Since K9 started deploying its teams, very rarely can "Charlie" attempt any of that silliness with any reliability or effect.

So that's basically the strategy and so far it seems to be holding up well. There really isn't any activity and God forgive me but sometimes I wish something would happen, just for the excitement. But, Ike and I settle in and try to become "tourists" in this beautiful tropical atmosphere.

But, that is the dangerous allurement of this duty, too. It's remarkable, that the perception of the same vegetation and scenery can be so different between the threatening nature of Viet Nam and the relaxing sensation of Thailand. While bathing in this hypnotic tranquil surface beauty, one can easily be swept under by the subversive dangerous undercurrent of the truthful essence lying just under the surface of this volatile area. I must be ever truthful and accountable to my faithful four-legged partner. There can be no room for failure. And, that is why I must start initiating a plan as soon as possible.

That opportunity comes the next week as I get to go to Bangkok on an errand for the Lieutenant and while I'm here I try to reestablish contact with "Nancy" and Sak.

I go directly to the international hotel and try to call "Joe" the cab driver with the number he had given me that rainy night, seemingly years ago. Someone picks up the phone but I cannot understand anything that is said by the woman who answers and she cannot understand me. I ask the desk attendant to try to interpret but that fizzles when she hangs up the phone.

"By chance would you know Joe?" but even the desk manager apologizes and can't seem to realize who it is I'm looking for, either. I try the taxi stand and for five minutes, I'm in the middle of six different opinions of whom I mean and none of them seem to still know how to get in touch with him. I really don't have much time for all this as I must get back to Utapoa by nightfall and it already is 2:P.M. I try to remember how to get to Sak's club, myself, but that doesn't work, either.

I can see that this is going to be a lot harder to get together than I thought. But, what else is new? I finally give up, this time, and grab a "Baht Bus" and say, "Bye Utapoa, lao, lao," to the driver. He smiles but seems to understand my very limited capacity to speak Thai.

Rain clouds begin to form in the northern sky as we head out of town on the primitive two-lane "highway". I see the passing scenery of peasant workers in the fields tending to their rice paddies and caravans of water buffalo and other vehicles trying to maneuver in this collision of old and modern technology. It's picture testimony to enduring determination of survival within the shadows of timeless temples and their proud ancient civilization. Truly fascinating!

By the time we arrive at the big sprawling base and man's new testimony to modern technology, it's raining pretty hard. I show the security my pass and I.D. and as I pay one driver I hail another from within the main gate to take me the rest of the way to the barracks. The front gate is always filled with people, either waiting to be allowed entrance to work their particular shift on the base or they're waiting for someone to come get them as escort. Along with the merchants who seem to sell just about anything, from live chickens to fake Seiko watches, which are called, "Main Gate SPECIALS" for ridiculous prices, that should immediately warn the buyer that they're fake, the gate looks like a "bazaar" of noisy activity and I must admit my pity and admiration for the job our sentries do. I wonder what would happen if they ever decided to put a K-9 team there. NO! I better not! Someone may try to do it!

I get back to the "house" and I still have about two hours before we take up our first patrol, here. I start to check my gear. Ike is laying on his bunk, listening to tunes on the radio and asks if I have anything to add to his letter to Luker, that he just wrote. He says he told him I went up to Bangkok. Just let him know I didn't get in touch with anybody as I can see it's going to be a bit harder than I thought, but that doesn't mean it won't be done. We'll get it done, with a little more time. Don't worry, buddy!"

I know that for any plan to be successful I must find our "ace in the hole", no matter what it takes. Sak must be found. I just have to allow for more time to find him. I have a lot of work to do.

I also ask for Susan and would he tell her what happened about not reaching her when I called that night and to give her my address.

Ike then posts it and says he would take it with us when we go to the mailroom on our way out to the kennels.

Chapter XXIV
FRUSTRATION

So here I am, once again, "walking the line" outside the perimeter of Utapoa, Royal Thai Air Force Base. This time it gives me the time I need alone, with King, to come up with a viable plan that, on the surface, has a working man's chance of succeeding. That's the difference between sentry duty and "taking the point," on patrols and re-con. On that detail, anything happens and mostly does. I wouldn't have the time I need to kind of sort out my options. They range from going A.W.O.L. with King, which is out of the question. That would only give those bureaucrats, back home something to gloat over and disgrace K-9 and "shooting" King, myself. Which is kind of not a consideration, since I'm trying to save the big guy.

I first can now intensively have King go into the new veterinarian department on the base and have him go through a complete check-up. He's never shown to be sick or injured in any way, but to be able to dispel any notion of a "dog virus" insinuation later on I feel can be most important. And, to prove "officially" him passing his physical can put to rest any other crap someone might be inclined to use against us, later. This will also give me an opportunity to gauge the new vet and see if he can be talked to.

It's amazing how all things can change when it can benefit one of these "gentlemen," in Washington. There have been a small number of dogs that have been allowed to come home after their hitch here were over but that was to only spearhead a recruitment drive, like Nemo or to focus attention on a politician's grand idea or plan of some kind. Then it was perfectly fine to have a dog come home. It just goes to show how much of a "threat" this so-called illness is to any of the dogs. The only real threats to any of these dogs are the heat for and the many snakes and insects that can attack in any remote part of this region. Especially in the high grass, jungles and swamps, where we go on duty. "Charlie" actually plays a minor threat since the dogs can usually detect them and alert us, before they can do much damage. Now with the word out about K-9's effectiveness and their "devil powers" most "VC" would rather just forget about any direct confrontation with the dogs. Booby traps and resulting injury are always a constant threat and it can't be anyone's fault or blame if one or two, with the many hundreds left by the "VC" continues to do its nasty work.

But, besides all the obvious reasons for a dog to get injured, in this war, it is usually caused by either neglect or lack of preparation. The constant threat of dehydration, especially in this hot, humid jungle climate is constantly rammed home to us by our supervisors before patrol. One thing in our favor is the moderation of K-9's working at night. But, unless left unchecked or carelessly miscalculated, the dogs would get through it. So I consider "official" documentation very important to ascertain and receive.

Now, I can also ask for help from my political representatives. Yeah, right! This is same Congressman of mine, Hugh Carey, who only two months ago turned down my request for a state flag.

You see, at that particular moment in the unit everyone still here came from a different state and someone thought it would be "groovy" if we all had our state flags to hang in our hootches to represent. Sounded great and even looked good as the various state flags started to come in. We even had a great time razzing' Cavanaugh, from Alabama, who received a flag the size of a handkerchief. Oh, the jokes he suffered! But, nothing compared to my response, when I got a curt three-line letter, saying "regretfully" they couldn't do anything in regards to my request since it was a "state" and not "federal" matter. It was signed by the "phony bastard" himself, proudly, on a pre-stamped letterhead. Everyone saluted and stood at "attention" as I made two holes in the response and hoisted it up the flagpole, alongside all the other flags. But, I made a solemn promise to return that letter to that bum, when and if I got home, with King.

For the next three days, I my post on the perimeter, and I could come up with nothing except for the fact that I was alone in this and could not expect any outside help.

As I rubbed King's head, I tried to put up a good front. I knew King knew, because I could see him actually letting down. His head and tail wasn't held as high anymore and his demeanor was lacking his usual cockiness and enthusiasm. We were running out of time and as man landed on the moon and the world rejoiced in it's magnificent accomplishment, I cursed those very same politicians and policy shapers who caused all this war's grief and misery for what seems to be their own "play-thing." They seem to be not serious in wanting to put an end to it. If they could put a man on the moon, why won't they stop this crap! I asked my big friend, "When did anyone ever see a politician leave office in any worse financial straits than they went in with? I always wondered why these, "servants" would spend millions of dollars for a temporary job, paying $60,000 a year. King didn't have an answer either. He just licked my hand.

It really frustrated me. When did these hypocrites get the power to do this? As "public SERVANTS and REPRESENTATIVES," they could order and direct their cigar smoking, cognac drinking careers to wealth and power and when they're through could be back patted congratulated with tributes and monuments to the testimony of their "greatness," to themselves. That's only after they make the obligatory world wind "concert" tour of celebrity speaker at some college forum, spewing out their version of the truth.

Everyone, it seems nowadays had their own version of the "truth". I wasn't trying to philosophize the world. I was just living it with the greatest friend anyone could ever want and all we were asking was to go home. Was that too much to ask for?

A few days later Ike comes over to me as I'm lying down.

"Are you alright?"

"Yeah, what's up?" I ask.

"It's you, man. Everybody can see it. You're losing it!"

"What?" I'm fine."

"Like hell, you are. Even the sarge asked me if anything was happening with you. Your face is in some kind of trance." Yesterday, man, Bobby was talking to you and you just disregarded him, like he wasn't there or something."

"What? I was talking to Bobby, yesterday?" "OH, man!" "I've got apologize to him. I don't even remember!"

"That's alright! I straightened him out but we're all concerned, man. Whatever happened to the man out covering each other's back? We got to stick together on this. It's all we got! You know this as well as anybody here, Dee. Hey, aren't we up for a pass or something, man?"

"I don't know, Ike. But, to tell the truth, I'm sick of going to Bangkok. I can't find the people I need to find and I just don't know anymore, man."

"Well, check it out, I got Luker the other day and he liked the idea of taking a five day "R&R" and I think that's what we need, man! This time we're going to this new place over-here called "Pataya"."

"Oh man, I haven't even called or written to Luker."

"Don't worry, I've been keeping him in touch with what's happening here and with you! He says he's going to kick your ass."

"Hey, Ike, you're good people, man. Thanks!"

"Hey, Dee, why don't you just let me join your little ditty, man. Who knows, I've got some connections, that might help."

"Ike, that wasn't even the case. We just didn't know you'd be for it, after your dog went down.

"Well, Dee, I knew it had to be something awfully big, to bring you down, like this. Even you can't take on the whole world, by yourself."

"I never claimed I could. But, I am running out of time and people who can and there's too much to loose. When is Luker coming over here?"

Chapter XXV
PATAYA

I didn't want to take off for the whole five days. If these were to be my last days with King, I didn't want to miss them for anything. Sometimes, I fantasized for something to go down so that King and I could go out, together. Then the realistic side took over and told me, somebody had to let the people know what happened here and I would have to call up the courage to "go home."

It was about two weeks later that I found myself, with Ike's urging, heading over to this "beach paradise," Pataya. We travel on a "Baht Bus," which is actually a small Datsun pick-up truck with two benches in it's flat-bed and covered by a canopy, holding six, but four decently. I only capitulated because of Luker being there and it would be good to see him, again, even though, I had nothing to report on any big "plan." I still only gave myself an overnight pass, as again, I wanted to get back to King.

The journey takes about 40 minutes to Pataya as opposed to the two-hour ride to Bangkok. I was pleasantly surprised to see how beautiful the area and surrounding landscape was and I even allowed the thought that at least King was here and not in the 'Nam. It really could be pretty good duty for him. Unless they start talking, again, about handing the dogs over to the Thai marines, this time, now.

It would be ludicrous to wonder, but sometimes, I think K-9 did too great a job, for these ungrateful bastards in power. In desperation and embarrassment to their "master plan," they just wanted K-9 to be dismantled and "go away," in the earliest shuffle. The dog's greatest sin was to do everything we ever asked them to do. Maybe, that wasn't the way the "script" was supposed to go. But, it did and now they're going to have to pay for it.

We enter this picturesque village, off the South Eastern coast and pass by the small seaside cottages and bungalows. Everyone is dress as they are on a permanent vacation, in summery white, baggy clothes and big hats to protect their eyes from the glare of the sun. Again, a clash of time warps is present as huge giant water buffalo vie for space with the tiny motorized automobiles on the narrow muddy roads of the village. Obviously, once a predominate fishing port, you can see the inhabitants now would love to turn this sleepy town into a close vicinity trade-off to the hustle and chaos of Bangkok, for the tourist trade. A smart entrepreneur with a vision could easily see the potential especially, if Utapoa, one day becomes an International Airport The roads connecting it to the ancient capital would become more modernized and more maneuverable. That two-hour ride could easily be cut in half. Then you would have this beautiful locale. But, first they would have to get a small thing, like the war, to stop. Shouldn't be something "money" couldn't accomplish.

We get to a stop and I see an American flag flying over this small but modern building with a parking lot in front. Two cars are parked in it. I kiddingly ask where they park the water buffalo but our driver doesn't answer me. Although, many Thais can't speak English, I've learned that many can and only fake they can't if they don't want to be bothered in conversation. I see a familiar face coming out the door and approach the "taxi."

"Luke, you look good, man" as we hug.

"And, you look like shit too!" he responds. "Com'mon in I got a cold one for you two boys, but *only* if you're old enough!"

"I'm gettin' older by the day, man. And, at this damned rate I'll be too old to take a crap for myself by next week." I respond. "But, a beer does sound pretty good, right now."

We unload our few bags from the dirty vehicle and it leaves, kicking up some dust. I stretch out a little and take in the breath-taking view of the beach and watery enclave, across the street from this government "exchange."

"Would anybody kindly tell me how did this building could find it's way into a place this beautiful"?

"No idea, but I don't ask questions like you do, man," cracks Luker.

"Glad to see some things never change." Ike says, "*I'll* drink to that," as we hoist up the cold lovely taste, only a beer can fulfill.

I mention Susan and Vanessa and he says that he spoke with Susan.

"She said she was home that whole night we last saw her and she knew that because she had gotten sick or something, and that she was in bed all night. But she also said nobody gave her any messages from you and, in the morning, when she called you nobody answered the phone."

"We were driven by the sarge out to the kennels, remember?" said Ike.

"He would be the only one to answer the phone, at that time. Everyone else is sleeping."

Luke continued, "She really thought you hated her for speaking out like she did. She really was heart-broken about that."

"I don't hate her!" I said. "God, I felt terrible about what had happened." "Did you make that clear to her, Luke?"

"Of course I did. She knows"

"Did you give her my new address?"

"Yeah, except...."

"Except, what?"

"Well three days later she got transferred along with Vanessa up to Da Nang."

"DA NANG! That red mud hell hole?"

"She kind of told me, that maybe it was better this way, for everybody. She just wanted you to know that she never wanted you to think that she tried to come in between you and King. She knew nothing ever would."

I kind of went into one of my moods with those words. How true and yet it all seemed so hopeless, now.

"You know, sometimes reality sucks!" We all drank to that, too!

After a few more beers, I ask another of my "famous" questions.

"You know, Luke, you seem to be pretty chipper and in lot better frame of mind, considering the situation we're in. And, knowing you feel just as strongly about this as I do…"

"Well, maybe, ol' Uncle Wayne, here, has an idea of his own".

I don't say anything, but I watch his face and I suddenly realize he does have something, "good," up his sleeve, by the sparkle in his eyes. He now picks up a bundle of the area's brochures, advertising the many hotels and nightclubs in the immediate area.

"Where are you guys staying? I'm staying at this one. It's quiet and comfortable. I got here yesterday, so I had a chance to check out some of the places, already."

He hands me a brochure and as I put it down on the table, he smiles a very big smile.

He forces the brochure back into my hand.

"That one's got a great supper show and all the girl's are beautiful. Just like the girls in Bangkok."

I now glance at the brochure and put it down on the table, again. Luker starts to lose his patience. I can tell he's busting a gut from laughing but I just don't get it!

"You know, Dee, you can be a real dumb bastard, when you want to be. But, that's ok, too. Just the next time I'll know enough to talk with King, because I know who really is running that show."

Continuing, Luke tries one more time.

"That place I just gave you to look at has these great red lights all over the place."

A "light" now turns on for me, a big "RED LIGHT". I immediately grab at the brochure, almost ripping it.

"Come visit Sak's place on the shore!"

"Oh, you got to be kidding!" I say, astonished to Luker.

"Oh, GOD!" I jump up almost knocking everything off the small table.

I look out the window at the sunny seascape, across the street as my eyes fill with tears.

"Thank You!"

We go over to Luke's hotel and sign in for a room for Ike and myself. I wash, shave and lay down for a rest on my room's very comfortable bed. I listen to the rumbling sound of the air conditioner's motors. I'm entering a very relaxing and stress-less state as I close my eyes. It s really been a long time for me to feel like this and I'm sorry now for not having more time, here, but, I know Luke and Ike can handle everything, if we get to see Sak. I can then go back and tell King the fabulous news. I also figure, now, I can always come back. As "heavenly" as this place was, now, it suddenly develops an almost "spiritual calling," for me.

The next sound I hear is the ringing of the telephone.

"Yeah, who is it?" I answer, half asleep.

"So do you want dinner or breakfast, in the morning?" I hear Luker.

"What? What time is it," as I fumble in my now darken room, trying to find the light and my watch.

"It's eight-thirty and you're going to miss the show, man."

"Where are you?"

"We're in the lobby. Get yer ass down here in five minutes or we're leaving."

"Where's is this place? You guys go and I'll meet you there."

"You can't miss it! Its two blocks up and on the outside is all red. Sak's name is in big letters outside. Dress casual, man"

"Ok, I'm just going to throw some water on my face."

"Needs more than that! See you up there."

I stumble over some furniture in the dark until I finally find the light switch. I'm in such a euphoric mood nothing really can get me "grumpy" on this night.

I get dressed in really the only clothes I own, next to my fatigues. I really ought to get some clothes. Now, Luker! He's a clothes freak. And, I notice Ike likes clothes, too! Real sharp. A fine clothes wearing man. They're always in the exchange looking at the clothes or in town getting measured for a fine fabric suit by one of the Indian tailors, to be sent home, "for a future day." Women notice and like that from a man. I must admit they got "style."

I get down to the lobby, now pretty much deserted, and I go out into the night. A beautiful refreshing breeze is coming in from the sea and I know my shoes, actually "hush puppies" is taking a muddy beating from the dirt street still moist from this afternoon's shower. But, I don't care.

I pass by some houses and casually glance to see the occupants going about their business or sitting down at the table talking. Everyone busy in their own little cocoon. Not really bothering about other people's situations. From the distance, I can hear the feint music being played on a radio, somewhere. Although, I don't understand any of the words, it's the mood, the melody and the rhythm that draws me to it. It verifies what we had discussed before. But, that's the kind of mood I'm in, tonight, a very peaceful, reflective, content mood. A frame of mind that allows me to see a common thread to everybody in the world. If only we allow ourselves to experience it more.

I finally get to this stucco two-story building with cars and people of all backgrounds coming and going. This is the "IN" crowd. The white walls are flooded in classic red lights, set in streams against the wall and accent the huge written red letters, "SAK's Place", very classy and very impressive. With all the activity surrounding it, it really has to be one of the busiest places in town. "Geez, I hope he remembers us!" as I start getting a bit nervous.

I open the big wooden front door and immediately get hit with a rush of warm air and smoke along with the sound of loud orchestra music. Many people are laughing and talking and just seemingly having a good time.

I can hear the unmistakable sound of a "big wheel" and a roulette table coming in from the first of the side rooms off to the left in the main vestibule welcoming area and I can see tables full of people playing cards in the room, off to my right. The second room on my left has the doors closed.

I continue to walk towards the huge darkened hall in front of me. Both doors are open and it's where most of the music and laughter sounds are coming from. A beautiful young Asian girl with long black hair walks up to me and offers me a drink from her pushcart type rolling bar set-up.

"I'm sorry, dear, he's already got one," as Luker, smoking this big cigar throws his arms around me in a hug.

"I never knew you smoked cigars, before," I say.

"Never did! But, look around. Everybody else is, too!" Sure enough, everyone was smoking a cigar! "It seems like the thing to do, partner. Besides, they're about the only thing in here that's free. Remember that, the next time someone wants to give you a drink. The tab will be waiting for you as you leave. And, baby it ain't cheap!"

"Where's Ike?" I ask.

"He's inside playing black jack and he's going to town, man. He can play!" We enter the room on where the people were playing cards and there's Ike having a good time with a whole bunch of chips stacked in front of him. He sees us and waves us over, smiling.

"Man, never been this lucky before!" I smile and give him thumbs up. I continue to scan the room for a familiar face in the crowd, but I'm not having much luck. I tell Luke that I'm going for a beer at the bar and just walk around.

"OK. I'll be here explaining this here game to Ike and give him all my expertise." I smile and comment, "Leave him alone. He looks like he can do alright all by himself."

I enter the now quiet and darkened main room, strangely reminiscent of the other club in Bangkok. The music from a wonderful melodic twelve-piece orchestra is playing accompaniment to a beautiful Thai singer singing a beautiful

147

Thai song. All eyes and ears give their utmost attention and respect as she sings. She really is extremely elegant and fits the clubs motif to a "tee." I must admit Sak has a lot of class and he likes his 40's style of big band entertainment, which is I feel unfortunately disappearing in the States. I feel, as if I can "groove" on this all night.

I now, however, see my target at the far end of the bar and I get all tensed up again. Supposes he refuses to help? What happens if he doesn't even remember me? Geez, why would he want to stick his neck out for us, with all he's got here to possibly lose?

"Oh, man!" I murmur to myself, as the girl standing beside me turns and smiles.

"Pardon me?" she asks. I just look real stupid at her and grin back. WOW! What a James Bond I am!

Blushing foolishly. I grab the bartender's attention and, so as not to disturb anyone, during the girl's song, I whisper to him to get me a beer and to buy Sak, at the end of the bar, whatever he's drinking.

"He's having an Amaretto on ice", mentions the bartender.

"Fine and start a tab for me, please."

"Sorry, can't do that unless authorized. Please pay, now."

I throw twenty dollars, American currency, on the bar, hoping not to look any further inexperienced and praying that it would cover this order and any unnoticed cover charges, that might be attached. I thank God when he leaves with the twenty and comes back with my beer, and even leaves change of some denomination in Thai currency. I know and I know, he knows, he could have taken his tip, paid off his gambling debt and gave his children their allowance for the month out of my change and I would have never known the difference. Or, would I have ever said anything about it, either. But, he turned out to be a good guy and by the end of the night we become real good friends.

That might also have been influenced by the reception I received from Sak, when he was handed my drink to him.

A person first meeting Sak has to be impressed with his style and demeanor. First class all the way and if he liked you, nothing was spared for your comfort or need. A seemingly pudgy man for his native Thailand but with a powerful round body, his always, smiling face covers up an intense and dedicated man, determined to be successful. Wearing his trademark red carnation in his white tuxedo and black pants, with his black shoes so spit-shine shiny it would make an army basic trainee die with envy. He's the perfect composite to Humphrey Bogart, in the movie, "Casablanca". Not a man to pinch corners when the cost is counted, but a shrewd businessman with always the eye out for the edge and future proposal. He carried a vision that could see the need and him wanting to be there to see it happen.

148

He now walked over to greet me with wide, open arms and a big welcoming grin. We hugged as the lights were coming up after the singer had finished her set.

"Oh so good to see you, my friend. I'm glad you finally found us. Don't you just love this place? Pataya is exquisite and what a future! Don't you think?"

"You took the words right out of my mouth, my friend. And God bless your good fortunes."

"Thank you, John. That means an awful lot to me, because you're a good man and, I know, you mean it. Why haven't you been here sooner? I told "Joe" to tell you where we were."

"Sak, I've been back and forth to Bangkok, since I've been stationed here"

"I know. Utapao" he says. "I thought you were mad at Sak."

"No! Never! Nothing like that! I tried to reach you, but I never made contact with "Joe" and I felt real bad."

"Never mind, you're here now, here, take my personal number. You have Sak whenever you need me."

"Well, I'm kind of glad you said that because"

"I know that, too. Not here, not now. Too many ears! We talk tomorrow in my office. John. We can do this, together. It would be fun!" A trembling came up my legs that congregated in my chest and struck out immediately to my eyes and face.

"Yes, it can be done".

"By the way, would "Nancy" be here?" I ask.

"NO, she left to go home to her family, oh, maybe two months ago. Fighting up there where her village is. She was a very special, girl."

We both smile and then greet the beautiful woman singer who now was gathering all the adulation and congratulating glances from the crowd where we were standing. All she wanted, however, was Sak's approval and attention.

"I haven't heard anything from her since she left. She was very special," he repeated, sadly.

He was THE MAN! And, he was my friend. I felt good, now, for the chances of my other friend, King. But, I wished I had gotten more of a chance to get to know "Nancy." Sak excused himself with his exquisite "trophy" lady and moved about the crowd, basking in his adulation and his celebrity status. I smiled for him and waved acknowledgement to him when he turned and yelled out, "John, 10 o'clock!" He then disappeared in the crowd and darkness of the club, once again.

The bartender refilled my glass of beer and wouldn't take my money for the rest of the night.

It was amazing for me to find how many truly beautiful women there are in Thailand and how they can all manage to step on your toes or stand next to you with their intoxicating aroma and beautiful bodies pressed up against mine. But for this particular night none of that mattered. I was just contented in remembering Sak's promised words of aid and assistance when it becomes necessary. I am also coming to see how thing's can be so temporary, just as fleeting as two ships passing in the night. A person must take advantage of what is there before it is gone. I just pray I can hang on to my partner, "this" one thing just a little while longer.

It was time to look in on my two "cohorts" and see how they were doing in the card room. I noticed a good size crowd surrounding the table where I left Luke and Ike and just held my breath for whatever it was, I was going to see. Much to my surprise and relief, Ike seemed to be doing exceptionally well. Looking over a few shoulders, I saw a huge stack of chips in front of Ike and he looked like he was having an exceptionally good time. Luker saw me and gets up from his seat next to Ike and comes over to me.

"Did you know Ike can play like he was born with a deck of cards in his hand?"

"No! How well is he doing?"

Luke says something astronomical and I start to laugh. "It's been a good night for K-9, buddy! A real good night, for a change." "We got a meeting with Sak, tomorrow, in his office, at Ten O'clock" "I don't want to miss it so I'm going to go back to the hotel, now." "Are you and Ike, ok?"

"Sure, man, we're cool." And don't worry we'll be there. Count on it!"

I respond, "I know I can, buddy."

Chapter XXVI
THE PAC

The next morning comes quickly and the bright sun shines through the closed drapes. It's 8:40A.M, still early. I had set a wake-up call for nine but I get up out of bed and take a hot shower. I call the main desk to cancel my wake-up call and order my favorite breakfast, scrambled eggs and bacon.

I'm in a great mood and all seems well with the world as I dress. After an invigorating hot shower and taste some of the just arrived cold orange juice that came with my breakfast order, I turn on the radio and search for an English speaking station. Not really expecting to find any. But, much to my amazement, I pick up a clear broadcast of an English accented man, forecasting the weather, from Singapore.

It's still quite unreal, sometimes, for me to comprehend some of the places I've seen and been to and the people I've met, all because of this war. I actually feel pretty good about what I've been able to accomplish within such a small space of time. When I think back to just year ago, being a "smart" punk, without a clue and the people I was with, although great people, but now, seeming so childish, I smile. I also gain a great new respect for my father, who I must admit, was pretty difficult, sometimes to understand and get along with at times. He did pretty well himself, for what he had to endure when he was my age.

Placed in a home for boys, because his family couldn't provide for all his thirteen brothers and sisters, being a good Irish Catholic family as they were, he forged his age at the age of sixteen, himself, and joined the Army, in 1915.

He used to tell stories of going down to Mexico, with OL' Blackjack Pershing and chasing Poncho Villa, "all over the goddamn hills and mountains" laughing like hell, at the many memories, I'm sure he remembered, but would never tell.

Rising to the rank of sgt., in an era when the rank of Sergeant meant you had to be a "tough sonabitch" shipped out with the highly decorated First Division, nicknamed the Big Red One, to Europe in 1917, for World War I. It was a hell of a way just to get out of the "house" and become a man.

Anyway, knowing, I've got to tend to "business," now, I finish getting dressed and then put in a call at the desk for Luker and Ike. After a few times and getting no answer, I wonder if anything happened with them after I left the club, as Ike really had won an awful lot of money, in the blackjack game.

"Shit!" I murmur, as I decide not to wait and leave early to go to the club for my 10 o'clock, with Sak.

The sun feels strong, already, for this early hour of the morning and it feels like the day is going to be a scorcher. The clouds mostly block out the sun during the Monsoon Season and rain and this causes an enclosed "greenhouse effect," making everything moist and damp, clammy and very humid. But, now as the English guy on the radio said, that effect will gradually withdraw as the seasons change. Great! Now it will be just blistering hot! Makes you wonder, which is the one you would rather have. But the village is so picturesque and the area so colorfully beautiful, I guess you just adapt and enjoy the area's other qualities and gifts.

I get to the big front doors of "Sac's Place" and they're already open as the day crew is busy cleaning up the place from last night's frolic. I go in and everybody is going about their jobs of vacuuming the beautiful red rug and mopping the white marble floor in spots where the rug doesn't go. This small army of men and women also clean and polish all the metal decor and big mirrors and stacks the glasses carefully at the bars in each of the three rooms. You can't say Sak isn't good for the economy in this otherwise sleepy town!

I can hear laughter and talking coming from the semi-opened doors of the fourth room, the ones that were closed last night. I walk over slowly and think I can hear Luker's distinguishable low pitch voice coming from within. I knock twice. I slowly and carefully open the door to find Luker sitting in Sak's chair with his feet up on the big oak desk and Ike sitting in one of the other deep plush maroon leather chairs in the office. They're still wearing the clothes they had on last night and each of them have a tall glass of champagne in their hands. I am simultaneously relieved and amused but also, so very reluctant to ask the obvious question.

"Yo, Dee! Welcome to "Ike's Place!" Luker yells laughing.

"If you ask real nice, maybe he'll let you mow the grass outside, after everyone else finishes what they're doing!" I look at Ike for any sign of normal explanation, but he's too busy laughing. Finally Ike says, "Dee, I couldn't believe it! I mean, I've done a little card playing before, but I've never had a night like last night, before!"

"How much did you win?" I asked.

"I don't know, yet. They're still counting it up with the two different currencies, trying to get an accurate amount."

"How about $25,000 U.S.," says Sak as he now enters the room, with both Luker and Ike jumping to their feet, almost falling down on their faces.

"Sit down, everybody," requests Sak as he greets me and shakes my hand.

"Dee, you didn't tell me about your friend, here."

Smiling, but not to offend, I say diplomatically, "I didn't know, either. But, I'm happy for the both of you."

"Oh? You're happy my house loses money?"

"No, not that way, but just think of the good public response, now, when the word gets out that someone can win $25,000, here. They'll all be here trying to win their share."

Scratching his brow, Sak finally says, "You might have something there! You know, you're pretty smart, boy." "How much you like to work for Sak, when you leave Army? It's beautiful area here! Good to live, after all the Communists die!"

Luker then says, "Maybe, you can open a club in the states? "SAK'S La-La," or something."

You know I just never knew how much I missed Luke, with all his "stuff." But, he just reminded me.

Trying to change the subject and get to the reason for this meeting, I cordially thanked him for his offer of "employment" and I would seriously consider it, but only after we attend to what we needed to do, NOW!

"Our time is getting short for any immediate moves. This all has to be done properly, but if all the pieces are available and in place, we just may make it."

"I already know what you want to do," says Sak. "I've talked with Luker and, although, I see it can be done, it won't be easy. Things move in and out of your base, everyday. But, your dogs are going to be hard to disguise without some "official" line or documentation to back up the move."

"I agree and I have an idea for that, too! But, I first needed you and to know I can depend on the "movement" itself. If I have you, we can then go to the second step. What helps us tremendously is that we have two of the dogs, here, already. We just need to get Luke's dog, Diablo, over here. We'll then have time for everything else to fall into place. Thailand is nowhere near the conclusion that Viet Nam is coming to. I see us here for a long time. Once the headlines of 'Nam disappear so will the microscope on this area. Our government is counting on it. That's why everything here is so permanent compared to 'Nam.

Sak smiles when I say, "Utapoa is being dressed up to be an International Airport and this area, in vicinity of the capital, is going to go off the map, as soon as some stability comes here,"

"Right Sak?" We both smile.

"Again, Dee, we work together!"

I counter, "Let's work together on this first to see if we have a marriage."

"Ok, deal!" Sak says. What do I do?"

"Right now, nothing but we're going to need transport to Japan for us and the dogs. From there we can then, hopefully, get them into the States, with our "official documentation."

Sak, says, "I can do that. We'll need some men, too, but that can be arranged. Leave it to Sak. But it'll cost a lot of money."

"Ok, tally up a figure for three dogs and two handlers, transportation from Thailand to Japan, one way."

"Three handlers!" says Ike. I'm in this, too!"

I hesitantly but carefully say, "We'll, to be honest, I was going to call Pete, Ike. It's his dog."

"I know," he responds, "but he may not be able to go. And, well, I need to feel I'm bringing "something" back, too." I don't argue and can fully understand his feelings. I look at Ike and he smiles.

"Sak, make that three, possibly four handlers."

Sak sits down behind his huge wooden desk and starts to figure out a cost.

"I make it out to be a whole lot," Luke whispers to me. I nod back, "We've got to see."

"Sak can do some things but it's still going to be a lot," he says discouraged.

"What's the price, Sak?" Luke asks.

"I'm going to need about $15,000, up front and the rest will take care of itself. But, I see another $10-15,000, to be safe."

"Geez, where in hell do we come up with that?" I say.

"You got a deal, Sak," as Ike speaks up from looking out the window. We all bow to Ike's contribution as our way home. K-9 never had a better moment, as my eyes fill and Luke hugs Ike.

"You know, this can actually get done!" Luker says.

"Good, it is done. Let's have a toast." says Sak.

The four of us raise a tall glass of champagne that Luke just poured and as we click glasses and drink, I feel pretty good. No regrets. And, a lot accomplished.

"Our next step is to get you over here, too!" I say looking at Luker. "All the dogs gotta be in one place and there is maybe one who can arrange that."

"Captain McKenzie!" The three of us say in unison.

"But, he's got to be leaving real soon." I say.

"Today, when I get back to Utapao, I'll drop in on the new Vet and see if the Captain holds anything over him. I'd like to work a transfer for "Blo" as soon as possible."

Luke then figures the obvious, "I guess I better be getting back to Tan Son Nhut, to wait for my surprise transfer."

We all agree and once more toast to the action we now have in front of us.

Chapter XXVII
TRANSFERRING DIABLO

It's about 4:30P.M. I arrive back at the sprawling Thai air base and I go immediately to see if I can see the doctor. Ike stays at Pataya for a few more days, taking care of loose ends with Sak. And, I tell him "be careful" playing any more cards. I look at Sak and he looks back at me. We smile to each other.

As I enter the hospital I see the doctor going over some notes he has written in a pad by the front desk.

"Sir, may I have few minutes of your time?"

"Sure, come on in, John. Is there problem?"

"Well, sir, I was hoping you would do something for me. Have you ever met or spoken to Captain McKenzie, over at Tan Son Nhut?"

"That's funny you should bring Captain McKenzie's name up. We went to the same Veterinarian school together and he was at my son's Christening. That's right, you came over from Tan Son Nhut a few months ago. How is Mac?"

"He's the best, sir. As a matter of fact, after a little conversation I had with him, I, all of a sudden, find myself over here with my dog and I've got to think he might have been behind that move."

"That would be like Mac, to do something like that."

"It happened so fast, I never really had the chance to thank him for what he was able to do for my dog, King."

"King? Good dog, that King. He's got a funny streak in him, but, I guess you know that."

"Sir, he's got a lot more than that, but that's for another time. I need to know if there could be another chance for one more transfer, before Captain McKenzie goes back to the States."

"I don't know," he says. "I would have to "request" another transfer to fill in a needed opening and then go through command for permission and then only if there was a slot created could a dog be transferred."

"Well sir, since the alert for insurgents, in this area, is still on and Utapao is at only 50% staffed, could you and Ton Son Nhut hook up one more time?"

He answers, "Well, I can give it try, but it has to be done this week. That's when Mac goes home and we'd have to deal with somebody else, maybe not so inclined."

"Sir, whatever it takes, please, and what ever I can do, please let me know."

"I'll need the dog's tag and name to go with the handler's. "I'll get on it first thing tomorrow. You've got my word on it."

"Sir, that's good enough for me and I owe you. Sir, Thank you!"

Thing's are really starting to happen, now, but I wonder if we still have enough time for everything. It won't be long for us to begin thinking about going home, ourselves. I feel that it might just be ok, for a little while at least, for the dogs to stay now that they're in Thailand. We won't be able to do anything else while we're here and we do have to leave officially and go back to the states, at the end of our tour.

What should happen then is that the dogs will be given to another American handler and that wouldn't be too bad for a short period of time. Besides, that would be a whole lot better than what was going to happen with the Vietnamese. So we've gained some time. Once things get set up back home and as long as the dogs are kept in good shape, we can then come back on our own for the dogs with Sak's help arranging the paper work for traveling internationally. A "clean bill of health" certificate is going to be very important for us to bring them home, too! We must also establish an "eye" here to keep us informed on how the dogs are and how they're being kept, until we can get back. I would think the Vet and a trusted new handler would be the logical choice for that.

So, I guess that would be it as far as a plan goes. It might not be much, but I for one felt a whole lot better, now, that I did a month ago. At least I knew we were going to do something.

The next few days passed with no word about the transfer for Diablo and I was beginning to get fidgety. I even started to try putting together another plan, whereas it would only involve Luker's dog, just to get him out of there. I just knew that with Luker out of the picture and on his way home, Diablo would be in a lot of trouble and we just weren't going to leave him there.

I wondered whether Sak could use his "magic" in Viet Nam. He said it would be a stretch but it might be done, if everything went the right way. Which meant more money. He said, there would be some people to "contact." I told him to keep it on stand-bye for the time being, but we may have to go that way if we don't receive any word from Luker, soon.

It came down the next night and the Vet happily gave me the news at the kennels. Luker and Diablo were finally, cleared, and were on their way. They would be leaving Tan Son Nhut and arrive here later on this very night, about 2:30A.M.

I was so happy I forgot protocol. I forgot everything. I just wanted to celebrate. Ike came over and was told the good news. We both hugged. That night on patrol even King seem to sense things were going to be ok, as he was his usual defiant self, again. Even stealing a piece of cake I so "foolishly" left on the rock, next to where I was sitting. As I patted him down and rubbed his head, I gave him some water.

There was a huge beautiful full moon out, breaking through the haze cover finally signaling the end of the Monsoon season. Some stars were even out. As I listened a little to the Armed Forces Thailand Network, I could really begin to enjoy this long year and all it brought. I thought about all the laughter and all the tears and I wonder if I will sound crazy if I tell anybody who would care to listen that I wouldn't have missed it for the world!

The glimmering moon covered the entire patrol area as if it were daylight. There was even a shadow on the ground. It was so bright. I felt so good that I even tried getting "Hanoi Hanna," on the radio to see if she was still up to her old crap, but I couldn't pick it up on my small pocket radio. I then tried Saigon radio and there was a very feint reception. Just enough to know something was there transmitting but nothing to listen to or hear.

I looked down to my big friend and said, "You know, buddy, that's the way it should always have been. But now, let's just call it a distant memory."

King stuck his nose inside the palm of my left hand, as he always does when he wants to agree with me.

We got back to the kennels, after our night tour and Luker was standing outside the air conditioned building waving at the truck carrying us all in from our posts.

"Ike is on the six-pack," I tell Luke as we start getting off. We hug and even King has a tail waving greeting for him. We're all pretty oblivious to everybody and I still got to bring in King to his house as everybody starts yelling they want to go home. I laugh but run King in and secure him to know he's alright, change his water and give him a patting down then run back out and jump into the six-pack with Ike and Luker and go to get some breakfast. Yes, scrambled eggs and bacon.

We stayed up most of the morning bullshitting and making plans to get down to Sak's place while trying not to wake anybody up, but being told to "Keep it down," many times, anyway.

It was good and it was the unanimous decision that "this place wasn't bad" meaning Thailand.

"I wouldn't mind staying here for another tour!" Ike said.

"I would have to agree with him," I said, but I don't trust Washington.

"Once they have your ass, here, how difficult would it be to send it back to Hanna. Especially, with your MOS, job description." Says Ike.

"Yeah, that job description, is a death certificate for us." Luke says. "Let them send their kids over here for vacation from college. They could call it the "Peace Corps" he said, as he became hysterical at his own joke and after drinking six beers and staying up all night.

I knew, then, we needed some sleep. I rolled over and turned on my little table fan and said, "That's it for me, kiddies." and, I went right to sleep.

The next few short weeks rolled by pretty quickly as we actually got ready to go home. "Charlie" never did make his anticipated entrance. (ed. note: Not until 1972)

I do feel good about actually leaving, yet, a distinct emptiness is in my heart. I try to rationalize that it'll only be a short separation, but I still don't like the idea of leaving King here a second longer than necessary. I could, however, only imagine the anguish I would be feeling, if I didn't know all that we have accomplished and have at the ready, when the proper moment comes.

Chapter XXVIII
GOING HOME

Ike, Luke and I check and double check to make sure that nothing can go wrong, but as our last patrol approaches, I'm still an emotional wreak.

I know everyone one of us that are leaving feels the same way but won't be the first to show it to anyone. That ride to the kennels is a very quiet one. No one has to tell me anything but, I can see a few guys ready to have a very "tough" night with their "buddies," for the last time. You just have to know these dogs aren't going to make it any easier. I will just say this. That night is one I won't share with anybody but with my big Best friend. It's that bond "thing," again.

Our replacements have arrived and already have taken to "making friends" with the dogs. I meet King's new handler and I seem to think he'll be ok, with King. I just tell him to do the right thing for him and to keep me informed on what's going on. He promises me he will and that he fully understands how I'm feeling, being King's only handler and trainer. He "won't disappoint me" and that he's "proud to have King for his new partner."

It was good for King to see me with the new handler and for me to introduce him to King. I would hope he would associate him, now, with me and that would ease the take-over process. I then look at King for one last time. I see him looking at me. Unashamed and feeling my face getting very red and feeling ready to burst, I turn and walk out the door. My tears are now rolling down my cheeks. And, I don't care! The only thing to grasp on to is that **I'll be back!**

That afternoon, with all the papers and signing-out over with, five of us board a C-130 and start to taxi out to the runway of Utapao Royal Thai Air Force Base. I know I'm leaving behind a huge part of me. Emptiness overtakes me. I look out one of the few small portholes as we lift-off. We're on our way to Tan Son Nhut, for our rendezvous with the other dog handlers we came over with, seven lifetimes ago.

As we circle, we pass over the K-9 area and for one last time I get a chance to see the kennels.

"I love you, buddy", I whisper to myself.

I then turn from the window and I catch Ike's face. It is very contorted and seems to be at it's breaking point. You don't need to say anything to someone who looks like that. You already know. That's when I hear Luker, on the other side under his breath, make his vow, "I'll be back!"

I grab his hand and bend over to Ike for his hand and confirm with forced smile and a wink, "Count on it!"

Two hours later we arrive and land at the big base in Saigon. Seems like not too much has changed in the couple of months since I was here, last. I ask if we have enough time to go over to the kennels for a quick hello but we're told we should be ready f or take off in about an hour, f or our trip to Japan. In the meantime, we could go over to the reception hall and get together with the others in our group, who are leaving.

A smile finally creases our faces as the thought of seeing some of the guys like Parker and Burton and DeWolf again, will be good to see.

We open the doors and hear a rumbling roar coming in from the welcoming room on the left. Luker opens the door and is ready to spring on some the guys we hadn't seen for a year ago. But these weren't our guys.

All these guys had smiling fresh and shaven kid faces and they all had brand new uniform fatigues, with bright shiny new insignias sowed on their sleeves. Right out of camp supply, never worn and a crease to die for. They're exuberance matched only by their sparkling spit-shined boots.

We excused ourselves for entering the wrong section and we can hear some heckling from a few about our "unkempt" appearance. Were we ever that "young?" We close the door and approach the other one. We open it up and see a few guys lying on the floor in the middle of the rotunda area and some more lying on the benches. A few are talking to each other in the window area and about twenty more or were just standing up against the wall talking very low.

"Luker! Dee! Ike Knowles! All right!" a smiling face and voice announces from just across the room from the door.

"Tom!" Tommy McDonald, I say! "Oh, man! How you doing?" We all meet in the middle of the room, hugging and smiling.

"We made it! Can you believe it?" Ha!

I ask where some of the other guys were but, there were just looks around to everybody.

"You mean this is it?" I say, incredulously.

"We had what 327 men with us?

"And dogs, man," adds one of the guys from the back.

"Yes, and dogs." "What's the count here, now, One hundred? One Fifty?" You can't tell me…

"Some are heading back from DaNang and will meet up with us in Japan, but there aren't too many in that group. Maybe Fifty.

"And no dogs."

"Yeah, And NO DOGS."

We all kind of reflect on everything and a huge silence fills in what should be a wonderful occasion. No one thinks it's so goddamn "Wonderful." It seems we all pretty much feel the same way.

"It's a pretty goddamn hollow 'victory' to win the way we were allowed to", said someone finally, echoing just about everyone's bitterness and frustration.

"Hell, they don't even want to keep the dogs. What are these people going to do with them, besides kill them", said another.

The absurdity of the whole thing finally pours out in the anguished voices of helpless brave men. They all start to shake their heads and tears well up in their eyes, questioning just one more time if there was one other thing we could have done for our partners and seeking solace in each other that everything we could have done was done.

But, that still will never Aleve the betrayal we all feel in failing them against this totally unexpected "enemy." It's very ironic but K-9 met and defeated every foe and obstacle it faced, except the one we never expected, our own country.

Ike finally nudges me and says, "You know I had my reservations, originally. That maybe we were going a bit too far in our plans, in actually "taking" the dogs away like we're planning. But, now, I'm proud we're going that one last step. Just look at these guys." Luke chips in, "I tell you what! Sak just may have found a whole new market to smuggle. And, he'd be a National HERO, in some circles, too!" I add. "Who knows, we'll tell him about it, but, let's get ours back, first."

A second Lieutenant pops his head in the door and announces for everyone to start boarding the plane. It's a sunny and very hot day and as we leave the hanger, I see the new guys heading over to get acquainted with their new home, for the next year. "Geez, they look so young," somebody says. "Yeah, and they don't even have dogs."

Our flight home from Japan was a pretty solemn event. I even heard one of the young stewardesses on our chartered commercial airliner conversing with her partner stewardess and remark about surprised she was about our very quiet behavior. She had reservations about taking this flight, her first taking home GI's, because of all the stories she had heard from other stewardesses and the chaotic conditions caused by the returning men. "These men look like they lost something. You would think they would be a little more happier about going home?"

Yeah, we're going home and the New York Mets are living a miracle year. You would "think" I would be happy.

Chapter XXIX
"WERE BAACK!!"

The next year or so is spent fulfilling our enlistment obligations. We've all been separated to the many stateside installations and our individual programs. Some of us still in K-9 detachments while others serve other military police situations.

Ike, Luke and I keep in touch almost weekly and we all maintain a direct communication with our replacement handlers. Pete, recuperating home and discharged, is recovering nicely and has been let in on the plan to get our dogs back and loves the whole idea. Even if we were to maybe fall off the schedule, he'd call and get us back on track. That's how involved he is and he can't wait for us to make our move.

I've been concerned from the beginning because, and I must thank my replacement for his truthfulness. King's appetite hasn't been good and he seems to lack an enthusiasm since I've been gone.

"He's pretty listless and really, all he does, it seems, is look out to the fields as if he's looking for something. He's lost some weight. I've had him to the vet and he checks out ok, and he treats me well, but he really misses you, man. You guys really had something special, together. You can tell."

I respond by just saying to, "Keep up the good work and it will be ok, real soon." Not that I don't want to, but I feel it not necessary to go into anything with him at this time.

The next couple of months past by so slowly and our only solitude is when we're on the phone talking to each other and describing what we have planned. Then it's all laughing and joking. But, we know, even with Sak, this isn't going to be easy.

It's in the next few months our cards are played for us. Quite unexpectedly, we receive the news that the order comes down to return all Viet Nam dogs, all the dogs originally embarked for Vietnam to be returned to Vietnam for "redistribution" in Viet Nam. This is the death sentence for all our dogs, we were afraid of hearing, from the beginning. Although none of it was necessary it seemed from all the excuses "why they couldn't bring them back," it was never even in the planning to bring these war heroes out and back home from the beginning of this magnificent experiment. That now some no-name bureaucrat in Washington just signed King's and all the other dog's death certificate and time had just run out. I wondered how the people who donated their dogs in answering their nation's call would have felt if they knew or even how well their dogs had served. We had to act or it would be too late.

I immediately call Sak on his private number. Never am I so relieved to hear a man's voice.

"Sowardee, Cop!" says Sak, in traditional Thai greeting.

"Sak, it's me, John!"

"John! Welcome to you! Very good to hear your voice, again. Dee, Moc!"

"Sak, listen, we have to get over there right away. It's very important. Is everything ready to go?"

"Yes! Yes!, Let's go. Do it now!" I relax a little, but I tell him, "Ok I've got to do one more thing, here. Then it'll take twenty-four hours to get over there. Unless you hear different, we should be there by the end of the week."

"OK! No.l! I be here."

My next call is to Utapao, itself and the infirmary. When a nurse answers the phone, she's kind of shock to receive a phone call all the way from the States and I can hear her stalling the telephone operator. I finally interrupt this debate on what and what can't be done, and just say to the nurse, "Please put your Vetinarian, on the phone nurse. I'm busy and I don't have all day." in my best imitation of an important blustery Washington voice.

It was the best I could muster up, without cracking myself up, in the process. I can now hear the nurse calling for "Dr. Tillman" and hearing her explain, she doesn't know who it is.

"This is Captain Tillman."

I now apologetically say, "Sir, This is John. Remember King's old handler?"

"Geez, John, of course, but how did you..."

"Sir, no time to explain. Are our dogs still at Utapao?"

"Yes, but they're going back as soon as the paperwork and transfers go...How did you know that?"

"Sir, it seems I'm always asking you for something, and I apologize, but how long could you stall that movement?"

"A week, maybe a little longer. But, John, It's no good. They have to go. There's nothing we can do about it, from here."

"FROM HERE, you say?"

"That's right," the Captain continued, "From what I hear everything's shutting down in Nam. There's a whole lot of confusion, if you know what I mean. As impossible as it is, it would still be easier to do something when the dogs get over there. There's still too much accountability here in Thailand. You'd be cutting it awfully close, but that would be your best bet, to take advantage of all the confusion, over there."

"Do you, sir, know anybody over there that can assist us?"

"There's a Vet, over there, I know. I can't speak for him and I won't give out any names, over the phone, but if I can get in touch with him he can do a few things. Call me back in a couple of days and let me see what can be done. John,

I'm not promising anything. But, I can certainly understand how and what you're feeling. I'm human too!"

"Sir, that's all I've ever ask anyone to be. I'll play with the cards you deal me. That's all I can ask. Thank You, Sir. I'll be in touch in a few days. God Bless You, Sir."

I immediately call everyone and offer the same opinion of the situation. We should get over there, NOW! We all agree as Ike, Luke and myself put in for an emergency 15 day leave, as soon as possible. The next day we all remarkably get our requests approved and all we need to do is sign the forms. Pete, as prearranged, will meet us in San Francisco and arrange passage on the earliest flight to Bangkok, Thailand. He never did say how he got all the money to pay for the tickets, always saying his "family" gave us their blessing, but, when we all arrived in the City by the Bay, he comes through by handing us our tickets.

I still was chuckling at the part on the "leave" forms we had to fill out and sign. The part that says that "the military disavows any responsibility to the person signing this leave for any life-threatening situations, illness or injury while this person is on leave, from active duty. And, that it is the sole responsibility of the signee to keep a proper conduct and discourse about himself at all times."

Smiling I asked the lady behind the counter, at the records department, what that could mean? Lowering her glasses and spying me very negatively, she says, "Oh, that's in case you get hit by a car or fall down the stairs and do bodily harm to yourself. Those things do happen, you know, soldier!"

"Oh, yes ma'am!" I respond.

"And what about taking on the whole goddam North Vietnamese Army?" I murmur, under my breath.

"What was that, you said?" she snaps at me.

"That would be a shame to ruin my rest, at home!" I quickly retort.

We all put down our home addresses for points to contact and our families are requested to just cover for us if there should be anyone that calls, but that really shouldn't happen, unless we don't come back. And by then, most people would know the whole story, anyway.

With a little time to wait for our overseas connection, we stop by our homes to pick up a few things and to say our good-byes to our parents while on our way to San Francisco. With Luke and Ike waiting in a taxi to take us to the airport, we've all been telling our families we're going to Las Vegas for a few days vacation. But, I don't think either of my parents believed me. You can always tell when a mom "knows." And, she can always tell when her little boy, isn't telling the whole story, too! I can hear a little quiver in her throat when the guys tap the horn on the taxi.

"Son, please be careful!" She always said that at moments like this, when she knew things wasn't what I was telling her.

My father hugged me and shook my hand.

"Dad, it's just something I we've got to do! Our friends need our help." I looked into his eyes. "I wish you could come along."

He smiled. "There would've been a day, you know…. Bring your friends home, son. They need you."

Waving back to them. I close the taxi's door. My mother turns to my father.

"They're not going to Las Vegas, are they?"

"No. They're going to meet their destiny!"

We all meet up in San Francisco and have a last dinner at this highly recommended Italian restaurant, by Pete.

"I hope they have pizza just a little better than the one we had in Bangkok," Luke says to me.

"Yeah, but you had to admit they had extra fine entertainment at that place." I add. "Our flight leaves at 10:00 P.M. and that gives us just enough time to eat and get over to the airport for check-in and boarding."

On the way we grab a newspaper and as we take off, we see the headlines depicting the rapidly deteriating situation and the "VC" going to hell with themselves celebrating up at "recently liberated" Que.

We can envision them moving down the "Ho Chi Mihn Trail," heading southward toward the dogs.

"It's going to be a bloodbath. And, nothing is going to stop the steam roller, this time, as it heads down the highway."

"Yeah they're better organized and confident than they were in Tet 68', when they tried to do the same thing."

"This time though the little people ARE rising up against the South."

"They see us pulling out and they want to be on the winning team. I can't blame them. Wouldn't you?"

Ike adds, "I just hope we're on the winning team, now!"

With our flight cocktails given us by the flight attendant we click our glasses to a toast.

"Ever since we joined up with K-9, it couldn't have come out any other way, my friends." I say.

"But, isn't that what they said at the Alamo." Pete says.

The three of us jump up and knock him down and start messing up his hair. One of the stewardesses comes over and asks to please cut out the horse playing. Luke, ever the man, replies, "I'm sorry for my fellow travelers, but, Ma'am, you've got the wrong species, it's DOG play." We again, click our glasses.

We all laugh. I remember the attitude we had when leaving Viet Nam. I look at our playing around, now, in contrast.

"Please, gentlemen, consider the other travelers," begs the stewardess.

Now, the Japanese stewardess asks, "Why the happiness? Where you are going there's a lot of fighting going on. Most people avoid going there."

Pete answers her very determinately, for all of us.

"Yeah, we know, we were there. We just left something behind and now, we're going to get it back." Pete has a "fire" in his eyes and I am extremely proud of our compact. We raised our glasses, one more time.

We eventually quiet down much to the relief of the stewardess and even fall asleep for a couple of hours. They woke us up for meal but, the pizza we had in San Francisco was still with me and I decided to skip the fish, or whatever that was they were trying to serve us.

"You know, I could use a little "home-cooking," when we get back." These restaurants just ain't making it."

"It's gotten to be that I even miss those C-rats we used to get on patrol."

"Man, that's hittin' rock bottom," says Ike.

"No really." I laugh, "They weren't so bad if you could heat it up." I say. "And they were just like Mom's cooking?

Oh, Man, please don't ever invite me to your mom's house." says Pete. "That's scary, man." Everybody starts laughing, again.

"That's cool, with me." I laugh.

Seemingly taking forever, we finally get the word to buckle our safety belts. We're coming for a landing at our destination, Bangkok, Thailand.

I look out the window and see a clear sky and some puffy white clouds as we start descending.

"Looks hot down there." says Pete.

"Well look at who wants to be a weather man." says Luker.

I know because I can feel it myself, but it's not so much the weather we're starting to feel as the pit in our stomachs. We get closer to landing. No one will admit it, as I watch their faces for any sign of changes of heart. Not one indication of wavering or weakness. Just a determined resolve now spreads across their face. It seems I'm not the only one looking.

Luke smiles at me.

"You know, I never brought this up, Dee, but you know your eyebrows, especially your right one, moves up and goes over your forehead whenever you get into one of your frame of mind or attitudes of determination and anger. It's your "evil-eye" that puts chills into a person looking at you, when you give them that look. Its your "Death Look", man. A man can read you like a book and he would be crazy to either disregard it or challenge it."

"I haven't seen it since the Ashu Valley. I would sure like to see it soon, brother."

"I'll see what I can do to make you happy, when the time comes." Is all I can say.

The tires of the plane screeches on the runway upon making contact with the ground, I might not show it for Luker but my heart does sings at how proud I am, again, for these guys and our noble crusade.

Chapter XXX
THE "TIGERS"

The plane finally rumbles to a stop in front of the receiving area of the main terminal at the Bangkok Airport. The door slides open and a dazzling mixture of heat and light come rushing in to the rapidly warming plane.

We all unfasten our seat belts and stand to stretch for a second. We have no luggage except each man has a carry-on backpack so that can eliminate having to go into the terminal and unnecessary contact with the Thai authorities. We hope to go unnoticed to the main gate and grab a "Baht Bus" and head immediately to Sak's place at Pataya. From there I can make my call to Dr. Tillman, at Utapao, for an update.

As we leave the plane and head down the movable stairwell, however, we all see a green military truck with a twirling red light on it. With its siren wailing it comes out to the tarmac where our plane has parked and comes to a screeching halt at the foot of the stairs. We hesitantly continue down the stairs but as we get to the bottom two tough looking Thai army men in sharp battle green jungle fatigues and black berets beckons us in broken English and gestures to get into the truck's rear compartment. We glance at each other very thoughtfully. I'm sure we all had the same fleeting idea. To either try and ignore these guys or, if they insist, maybe overpower them and take their truck.

"May I help you, sir?" I finally ask. "Is there a problem?"

All kinds of thoughts run at light speed through my mind at what this can be all about. Can we set off an incident, here and now or can we be denied what we came here for. No, not now!

"Please, no trouble, you must come, now. Very important!" I look around and see the flight crew and the stewardess up on the top rung of the stairway, looking at this whole thing. I'm getting real annoyed and I can't even begin to believe this is happening. Did they call them? How did anyone know about us? And, what do they know?

"Can you tell us where you want to take us or we're to see?"

"We take you to Sattahip Harbor." says one of the men. "Please, no problem, we go, it's getting late!"

"Sattahip?" "No Bangkok, No Police?" I ask.

The two men start to laugh.

"No, Sattahip. Boat waiting!"

All of a sudden a light goes on in all our heads. "SAK!"

"Yes, Sak. Please! Bye Lao lao, we must hurry".

I turn around and smile at the flight crew and at the stewardesses and they wave back. Luke gives them the "thumbs up" sign.

We all get on board the truck and speed out the front gate of the airport. Once on the road we head toward the highway that leads to the South. To Utapao. To Pataya. And, to now, Sattehip Harbor.

The driver drives like a mad New York City cabdriver, without a tip. He swerves around and blows past other vehicles, people and big animals with his red light and siren wailing. I just wonder if any of these water buffalos knows the rules of the road. And who ultimately has the right of way. That would be an interesting headline in the newspaper. But, then I also remember that the military "wouldn't assume any blame or responsibility" with that waver I had to sign for that "records" lady. Wouldn't she be all "broken up" about that!

With all the times I've traveled this very same road and see all the familiar landmarks, I know at least we are heading in the right direction, even as we wiz by at this ridiculous speed.

An hour passes when we get a call on the radio, spoken in Thai. One of the soldiers picks up the headset and speaks briefly. He then turns and hands me the microphone.

"Hello?"

"Ah, my friend, this is Sak, welcome home!"

"Sak! I'm glad to hear you! This was a surprise. Who are these men?"

"John, we have good fortune! These men are a part of a special group of people who are here to help us. I will introduce you to my brother, when you get here. But, time is running out. The Cong have already entered DaNang with the Russians and are already occupying the harbor. As we speak, they are now attacking Pleiku. There's no real opposition and they are steam-rolling to the Delta. Only Saigon is putting up little resistance. We've got to get over there, now, or it's too late."

"Sak, can these men be trusted?"

"YES! They're the Tigers, John. NUMBER ONE!"

"The Tigers?" I respond. "Sak, we should be there in about thirty-five minutes. Sattehip Harbor?"

"Yes! Come quickly. We'll be here."

"Geesus! The Tigers!" I hear Pete say, and I smile. "Sak always had CLASS!" I say.

"Cop," which means "sir" in Thai, "Cop!" Can I get a landline on this radio? I must make a call to Utapao."

The soldier not driving, reaches for the monitor set and turns the dial to the left for another frequency on the radio.

"Call, now!"

"Utapao, Utapao, this is frequency 1350"

"This is Utapoa, Security Police 635th. Who is this?"

I decide to use our old calling sign, hoping it would still be remembered and honored.

"This is Tiger Flight, 635th Security, K-9, please put me through to the infirmary, Dr. Hillman."

Some seconds pass and then I hear the doctor's voice on the cracking speakers.

"Captain Hillman."

"Sir, this is John!"

"John? You just pop up anywhere! How do you do that?"

"One day, sir, we'll all sit down over a beer and I'll tell you, but right now, where are the dogs? And, are there any status changes?"

"The dogs left last night. It was the longest I could delay the move. They're all back at Tan Son Nhut, and I guess you know what's happening over there, as we speak.

"Did Saigon fall yet?"

"No! Not yet! They're buying time for the Embassy staff to get out and it seems "Charlie" is content to sit on the doorstep, for the moment."

"I contacted the base doctor at Tan Son Nhut. All the other dogs have been turned over to RVN, already."

"What RVN?" Captain, you know they're all dead, already."

"I don't know anything. But, with your three dogs, the vet, over there, got three options. He can kill the dogs, himself. Turn them loose in-country. Or, use our plan. That's to put them to sleep and crate them up for travel at the kennels using the deuce1/2. That's if he gets my call back. He would give me to the last minute before he decides, what to do depending on what I heard from you.

"Sir, then please call him, immediately. We just landed and we're here in Thailand. We're going in to get them out of there, now. We need just a little more time."

"Then get off my line before he evacuates. John, Good Luck! Bring those dogs home, Sgt."

"Thank you, sir!"

The line goes dead and now, we just hang on till we get to Sattahip. Nobody talks but I see the determination on our faces. Lips are tightening and their eyes crisp and sharp. It's a good feeling!

We see the water as we approach the coast and we know Sattahip is just around the curve. We come to a clearing and see the ancient wooden houses and people scurrying around like K-Mart, having a "sale." As we arrive at the pier area, now, we see a big bellowing cloud of smoke and an old freighter with one stack. Looks like an old World War II "Victory" ship. Black paint has been used to cover up the many rust spots on the hull, but, for right now, she looks like "home."

The green truck, with it's red light still flashing slams to a stop at the boarding gate and I can see Sak standing there with another man, in a black beret. Wearing his uniform and having his arms clenched behind his back, he looks like the boss.

"John, my friends, this is my brother, Captain Nugyen. He's a commander in the Royal Queen's Guards, The Tiger Division."

I hear Luker whisper, "They're considered by many to be the best single fighting force in the world."

I reach out my hand and we shake. A good firm clasp and I smile. "Nothing weak with this guy" I think to myself.

"Sir, I am honored and am eternally in your debt."

"It is me to have the pleasure, May I call you John?"

"Please!"

"My brother has told me about your situation and although in my country we don't look upon dogs, especially. I can totally respect you and your men on your mission to help your friends and partners. We have that loyalty in our force, as well. My men and I can understand your feelings. You have my most trusted twenty, hand-picked men and myself at your assistance."

With no moment wasted, we board the boat and, immediately cast off from the dock. Sak waves to us "good-luck" from the wooden pier.

"We have big celebration upon your return, my friends."

I turn to Captain.

"Sir, you know the situation we're going to face over there?"

"Yes, probably better than you do. We've been listening into the radio calls coming out of Saigon. It's sounds like they've just started the final shelling, now. Charlie is good but they're drunk with success. They're not expecting any resistance. We can get in, make a quick strike and get your friends. We should have a good chance to take advantage all the confusion and celebration and get out before they can reorganize a defensive strategy. Charlie is tough, but we fight them before. My men, however few, are better."

"Captain, I like the way you think."

Can I honestly allow myself to feel, now, with these guys we really do have a shot at this?

About an hour passes as we head for the rising cloud of smoke and fire we all can, now, see off in the distance.

SAIGON. It's taking a terrible beating. Almost as if it were a payback to a debt it doesn't owe, for all the frustrating years of fighting this tiny country has had to endure. What a terrible price to pay because of outside meddling, interference and domination.

My thoughts are broken by a sound behind me.

"Luke?"

"You've been pretty quiet, lately. Having second thoughts?"

"Na! I had hoped it wouldn't have to come to this, but, here we are."

I ask him, "What about you?"

"NO! Not at all! It's just too bad that the real bad guys aren't even here. They always get away free, don't they?"

"Not this time, if I can help it." I say. "If we get out of this, this story must be told. The country must be told about our dogs"

"Ha! I see your "evil-eye" working just fine," As I now, for the first time, feel my right eyebrow crawling up my forehead.

"Well, then, we have to show the people who we are" a voice coming from behind Luker, says.

Ike and Pete are already wearing their berets, with K-9's dog insignia on it, boldly marking the crease.

"Looks good!" I say as I'm handed mine by Ike.

"Yeah, it's about time these "Zips" get a good look to see what K-9, can do up front and pissed off, in the daylight!"

"Yeah, it'll be good for them to see K-9's faces, instead of just our shadows," says Pete.

Our destination gets nearer as the smoke intensifies and the smell and the noises of the mortally dying city attacks our senses. The Tiger commander comes over to us and announces that we're entering the harbor, now.

"Keep an eye on the dock for any movement. There shouldn't be but just maybe some deserters or advancing troops have already taken up positions, there."

He then gave us what we were going to need. We slipped into some green camouflaged fatigues and jungle boots. We were then given our weapons, to be carried and concealed in the huge backpacks and green duffel bags. M-16's, with adaptor grenade launchers, a bag of twenty round clips and bayonets. We strap grenades around our waists. I then turn to the Thai commander, "Captain, you're officially "neutral," in this. You and your men should stay behind on the dock for as long as you can."

"I understand, and agree, but we'll set up a perimeter defense at about a hundred yards to cover your return."

"That would be great if you would do that, for us."

Ike now speaks up.

"Me and Pete talked about this before. It's Pete's dog so he should go. I'll hang loose and help coordinate your return, from here. Just stay on the radio so we know what's coming in with you."

"Thanks Ike. Don't worry. I'm sure we'll have enough for everybody, when we get back."

"Hey, Luke, we got our "music" for the ride back? We might need some sweet tunes, man? Always got to have the music"

Luke acknowledges, "Got them right here, partner. They'll do the trick."

"Well," I say looking at everybody, "It looks like we got ourselves a plan!"

As we get closer to the wooden pier, we know this is for real and for all the marbles. They'll be no backup or support. I wonder how they'll tell it in the newspapers, back home. And, I also wonder what some people in Washington will say over their coffee and cocktails.

"OK. LET'S GET OUR FRIENDS BACK!"

Not a sign of anything on the dock. The big boat slowly and noiselessly coasts up to the wooden slip and brushes up against it to help it stop. The ship's landing plank swings over the side and swiftly gets tied to the landing strip. Some of the "Tigers" jump off and immediately secure the rest of the lines of the boat to the pier, then take their positions along the strip. The three of us, Luker, Pete and me jump off and upon landing on our feet, in the mud on the dock, head off through the surrounding jungle, towards Saigon.

The moment Dee, Luker and Pete disappear through the jungle curtain, Ike and the Thai commander look at each other. Without a word spoken, a deep sigh, comes from both of them. They know what has to be done, to get ready for their upcoming party. Late afternoon is fast approaching and they know they didn't have much time to do it. The Tiger commander starts barking orders, in Thai, for his men and without a moment's hesitation, his men go out to do it.

Ike heads directly to the base road that connects the sprawling airbase with the dock. He knows Dee had planned to use that road and he probably would be bringing a lot of angry people with him. He succeeds in communicating what his plan is with the four Thai marines with him and they begin to chop down the trees at the point where the road meets the opening to the harbor area. They then saturate the entire area with as much gasoline as they can find on the dock. They then rejoin the others in digging small ditches strategically around the area of the harbor with the whole system linking itself back to the ship.

The Tiger commander is on the bridge and Ike can see he is holding off the anxiety building up in the ship's captain. The captain wants to leave now but the tiger is assuring him it would all be all right.

YEAH, SURE! Even Ike wasn't going to buy that. Starting to get dark now, and everyone knows if it was going to happen it is going to happen soon.

Everybody stops what they were doing when the first sounds of a truck is heard and is coming towards the harbor. The only problem is the sounds are coming from another direction and not from the base road. Finally, the beam of the headlights show themselves splitting the rapidly approaching night and we all know we have a problem. Everyone gets down and holds their breath.

A command jeep and three formerly American Army heavy trucks slowly appeared, with unit decals still on them, but, now, filled with uniformed North Vietnam Army regulars.

Ike just shakes his head in disgust. But, with the way we felt, about how things were, it was very appropriate, Ike reasoned.

The four-vehicle convoy enters the area and circles up to the pier stopping next to the silent and seemingly deserted ship. Only the smoke from the old ship's stack shows any distraction to a completely deserted area.

The two in the command jeep stand up and as one surveys the area through his "brand new" U.S. decaled binoculars the other yells to the ship for anybody on board to show themselves. These NVA just didn't believe they were going to run into any resistance and really didn't show much immediate concern for the situation.

Thank God, for that. It was just at that moment, we could hear the shooting and explosions and the blaring of music, coming from the base road. And it was getting lauder. Ike immediately knows who is coming and something has to happen, now.

A single shadowy hand reaches up over the ship's railing. With a single shot from the pistol, the commander in the jeep, the one with the binoculars, falls slowly down into his seat. Almost simultaneously the area blows up to screams and explosions.

The third vehicle, the second truck, blows up with all on board into the air from a thrown stick of dynamite finding it's mark. At once, all the NVA soldiers jump off their remaining three trucks and start shooting wildly in every direction. They can't see the Thais and really are doing more harm to themselves, shooting in crazy desperation than being an effective fighting force.

Hearing the chaos getting lauder and approaching the area, Ike and a couple of marines get over to their designated spots to welcome their friends and the dogs. Seconds later, a familiar dusty behemoth comes flying out of the jungle, half shot up but without any intention of stopping for anything.

With that grand entrance, Ike now gives the signal and immediately a flare ignites the gasoline saturated trees and bushes, blocking the entrance to the harbor from the pursuing enemy soldiers.

Joining the other marines, they now head for the ship, with each trench covering for the men who have just past them by. In some cases, however, some straggling Vietnamese just happen to reach an area and intersect with the retreating Thai commandoes. It was more to their bad luck, if this is to happen, however, as the Tigers are in full control and the Vietnamese are more in leaderless confusion. Hand to hand fighting does break out in isolated areas. It's just for sheer numbers that the Thai Tiger forces are getting pushed back.

As soon as the commander sees the three wooden boxes and Pete laying on top swing on board the lift on the ship, and Dee and Luker helping each other up the plank, he blows the ship's whistle and all the tigers now break-off the fight and climb back on the ship.

Bullets and explosions rip into the old boat, as it slowly leaves the pier.

Pete is still on the skiff, with the three boxes, as he lays motionless on the main deck. Dee and Luker remain on the deck where they landed in a bloody huff.

Ike gets up into the captain's bridge and gets on the radio for any kind of assistance-*S.O.S.*-appeals.

The ship is all pocked marked with shot marks, but slowly the fighting subsides as it moves out of firing range of the small weapons fire from the pier. Just as an eerie calm settles the ship, it almost suddenly capsizes from the cannon fire coming from the now fast approaching three harbor patrol boats. Ike is still on the radio requesting any kind of intervention or assistance for the ship carrying neutral Thais and wounded American refugees.

"IS there anybody out that can help us, from this attack? This ship really can't take much more of this barrage."

Seconds, seemingly pass like hours, when a crackle is heard on the radio.

"Hold on there, partner, we'll be there in two. Give me your coordinates, again!"

With the sound of a whoooooosh the first rocket flashes across the water and fires into one of the harbor boats. A second rocket blast from the now fast approaching apache helicopters makes the surrounding water rises up violently and seems to swallows up the second patrol boat.

Everyone, on the small freighter cheers and hugs each other for their luck. Whooping and yelling, all the men can appreciate how close they came to disaster, and not the success that now is apparent.

Ike, hugging the Thai Captain, comes out of the bridge and takes a deep breath. A smile of complete satisfaction covers his face. He now wants to join the others in celebration.

It is as he climbs down the ladder, he is not hearing what he feels sure he should be hearing. There's no cheering or celebration. Instead of seeing 30 men jumping up and down hugging and dancing, all he sees is men standing around, and heads bowed. Not believing what he is seeing, he watches as some of the

Thai marines gently lift Pete up off the boxes and lay him down on the spread out blankets on the deck. He's not moving and can hardly believe his eyes as they now cover his face with the top blanket. He frantically runs over to where Dee and Luker are still laying on the deck. Dee rolls over and sees how badly Luker has been hit. It looks bad.

"We don't have a doctor on board this trip, Luke"

"That's OK. I figure I don't need one. Funny, I didn't think this was going to be the way."

"How are you?" he asks.

"I'll be ok, a few cuts and bruises."

"Dee, you never could drive worth a shit. I should've done the driving"

"Maybe, next time"

"You can bet yer ass on that. Bring our dogs home, brother"

My eyes fill up with tears, as Luker becomes silent.

He now hears more commotion over by the skiff, where the dogs are. Ike runs over there and get s hit, like a brick wall in his tracks. I attempt to get up but Ike stops me.

"What's happening, Ike? TELL ME, Damn-it!!" sensing something terribly wrong.

I can see Ike rolling back his eyes, looking to the sky crying. I can see Ike looking at me with an unbelievable look of desperation and helplessness, now kneeling face down.

Not having to ask, I drag myself over to the boxes. Some men help me stand up.

I now see the blood seeping from the crates and I immediately attack the wooden planks on the sides to get at the travel kennels our dogs are in. I'm screaming and cursing, out of my mind with fear and dread. Through tear filled eyes I order the boxes to be opened at once. This being done, I see Pete's and Luker's blanket covered bodies off to the side and can't believe this nightmare I'm trapped in.

I shake my head in denial, opening their crates. I can only pray Diablo and Ranger didn't feel anything in their gentle sleep.

Ike just sits down shocked and cannot say anything. He just stares out to sea in a blank expression.

A couple of Thai soldiers finally rip open King's crate. I am shaking with desperate helplessness as I open his kennel door.

I see King lying on his side. The inside of his box is bloody. I yelled for help. He is still alive but laboring heavily in trying to breath. With him twitching and jerking uncontrollably, I called his name. I see his tail trying to rise very weakly. I press a cold cloth on his head, the same head, I always patted. I know he likes that. He opens his eyes and looks at me. He weakly licks my hand as if he had been waiting for me to come back.

His big brown eyes close and, then, all movement stops.

ADDENDUM

Some years later I happened to be in Washington, DC. I was visiting a friend who was attending college, there. I remember the day as seemingly just the antithesis to what the weather had always seemed to be on the other side of the world, so bright and a cool October wind blowing the autumn leaves giving electricity to the air.

We rode in the car circling the city of monuments and tributes to itself. The breath-taking sites of the Capital Building, The White House, Washington Monument and the Lincoln Memorial made one proud to be a part of the American Society. It was decided after lunch we would travel to Virginia, just a little hop over the bridge, and visit Arlington National Cemetery.

It was there that President John F. Kennedy and his brother, Sen. Robert, was buried. My friend had a class project on their heroism, contributions and sacrifices these two men gave to their country.

When we left the car parked, you could immediately feel a special quality of revered atmosphere and almost awesome solemn respect that fills the air.

We walk and walk surrounded by magnificently manicured lawns and immaculately kept headstones of war veterans who gave their beloved country the ultimate sacrifice. It was as if we were in a church. We didn't even talk to each other for respect and not to disturb this peace, these men and women had earned.

Passing some other visitors on the concrete walk and being just as solemn, we approached the Eternal Flame, that marks the resting place of our thirty-sixth President and his brother. We acknowledge some other visitors and silently say a prayer then continue on our narrow walkway to visit the other section of the Cemetery.

Funny, but now, after paying your respects to the President, it seemed OK to speak a little and express our, up-to-now, suppressed inner thoughts.

Immediately, we compared thoughts and ideas, and even opinions of the two men, which may have conflicted a little. But, as always, the inevitable question always comes up, "Where were you, on that day"?

After she goes first and tells me some things about school and her mother taking her shopping for her first something or another, she now smiles and says, "OK, your turn. Where were you?" it's meant as a harmless question and no subjective or underlining thought is construed. I smile when I remember being in school that day. The vice-principal came over the loud speaker to announce the day's instructions. As this was a Friday, it was also to give us the weekend's activities to be "attended," in supporting the school.

It feels like "four" lifetimes ago and how simple and easy it all seems now.

It was, however, until I remembered where I was for Bobby's assassination, that June night in 1968, California, I remember being with King, jumping and playing and running around, and me trying to catch up and train him.

I become silent and my mind floats away for a very special moment. And, my eyes start to swell up with tears. My friend immediately touches my hand and says, "Geez, John, I didn't know you liked Bobby that much."

That got me back to the present, in a jolt! Now, smiling and brushing away some tears, I say, "No, not that Bobby wasn't Ok. No, it was something else that was happening that I kind of don't talk too much about."

"Oh, I'm sorry, I didn't mean..." "No, of course not."

A few minutes past and we continue down our winding path, but now I feel she is blaming herself for "ruining" a great day and I now feel I owe her an explanation.

We get to a section where I see memorials and different commemoratives being honored, for military service. I say, "Let's go in here, I want to show you something."

As we go further on this new trail we see many monuments and remembrances to companies and outfits of soldiers and just mostly about everything you can name that would be connected to war memorabilia.

"You may not know this, but I was in Viet Nam." I say finally. "I'm hoping to show you something, here. It's got to be around here, somewhere," I say most assuredly. "John, you never said anything about being in the war? Where were you? You came back all right. Did you see any fighting?"

I smiled but all I said was, "It was OK," still looking for what I wanted to show her. As we kept looking, she continued, "Geez, I know some guys who say they were there and they're all messed up in the minds. I got a guy in my class and that's all he talks about. That and drugs. But, you seem...."

Again I smile. "Yes, I'm fine." But, I'm really getting a little frustrated not being able to find what I wanted to show her. "John, I think we came through here before. I remember this statue to Florence Nightingale, from before. She's right and I sit down on this bench for a second. My friend comes over and sits next to me, sensing my frustration and surprise at this outcome.

"I just wanted to show you what I did, overseas." "That's Ok, maybe there isn't anything, here, for it, John." "There **SHOULD** be!" I said, getting angry, at the thought.

It was getting cooler and the shadows of the trees started overtaking the daylight as the evening was fast approaching. I said I was "sorry," to my friend, and suggested getting back to the hotel for our planned dinner, that evening.

As we were leaving the park, I walked over to a park ranger standing by his station as I just wanted some information, and if he could be of assistance. "Sir, would you please tell me where the K9/War Dog Memorial is located?" I could see my friend's startled reaction. She had never heard about K-9 or war dogs. But it was the ranger's reaction that surprised me.

"WHAT?" "DOG Memorial??" He was laughing and thinking it a joke. He answers, "We don't have any dog statues, here. This is, after all, ARLINGTON NATIONAL CEMETERY!" still smirking.

He calls over his partner and asks him if he ever heard of a "dog statue," or something. "OH, yeah, isn't that the one over there by the tree?" laughing at his own joke. They stop very abruptly when they saw my face, as my right eyebrow start to rise up over my forehead.

My friend, feeling my body getting very tense under my sweater suggested we go, "There's nothing here for us. Let's go, John."

As we turn away and walk over to the car, the ranger's taunt seemed to follow us. "No animals in here, they're not allowed." Suddenly a small rubber ball comes bouncing, seemingly from nowhere and lands at my foot. A big, strong, beautiful tan and black German Shepherd approaches us on the run. He stops at about five feet away and with his tail wagging, friendly, gives me a happy bark, "telling" me to throw the ball. I pick the ball up and seeing his people in the distance, I throw the ball. The big fella immediately turns, on a dime and runs off, only to abruptly stop after about five feet. He turns back to look at me and gives me a facial "smile." A very familiar "smile," then runs off after the ball.

"Did you see that?" my friend asks, astonished. I smile, then, looking back at the two guards, I vow, silently, "*I'll* **be back.**"

There have been rumors, that of the over 4,000 war dogs that served in South East Asia, during the Vietnam conflict, only 172 could be smuggled back into this country, after the war.

To this day there is not a single National Memorial or Commemorative to honor their achievements, valor or sacrifice given by this Nation to it's K-9 soldiers.

We are the only nation in the Industrial World not to do so.

Sgt. John E. O'Donnell

ABOUT THE AUTHOR

The author is presently a life-time member of the Vietnam Dog Handler Association. He has also created a traveling exhibit and he along with other fellow dog handlers attend and are available for speaking engagements to make aware K-9's many accomplishments and acts of heroism and to solicit the public's support for their petition for a national commemorative memorial by this nation to honor the WAR DOGS.

THE BATTLE WILL CONTINUE!

When that day eventually does come, it will be the author's dream to go back to Vietnam and bring back the remains of some of these American dogs, left abandoned, and properly inter them where they so rightfully belong, HOME.

Since no corporate entity has yet responded to our call for help, or with contributions to the cause, you can make a tax-deductible contribution to assist in our goal of erecting a deserved and fitting memorial to these true American war heroes. Your support would be most appreciative.

War Dog Memorial and Education Fund
PO Box 475
Kearney, NJ 07032

You can visit the author's web site at http://www.wardogmemorial.com and the Viet Nam Dog Handler Association website at http://www.vdhaonline.org for further information on future exhibits and functions.

CPSIA information can be obtained at www.ICGtesting.com
Printed in the USA
BVOW041925200313

316039BV00001B/30/A